Oriens

ORIENS

A PILGRIMAGE THROUGH ADVENT AND CHRISTMAS

(December 3, 2023 – February 2, 2024)

FR. JOEL SEMBER

OSV

Our Sunday Visitor
Huntington, Indiana

Nihil Obstat
Msgr. Michael Heintz, Ph.D.
Censor Librorum

Imprimatur
✠ Kevin C. Rhoades
Bishop of Fort Wayne-South Bend
March 17, 2023

The *Nihil Obstat* and *Imprimatur* are official declarations that a book is free from doctrinal or moral error. It is not implied that those who have granted the *Nihil Obstat* and *Imprimatur* agree with the contents, opinions, or statements expressed.

28 27 26 25 24 23   1 2 3 4 5 6 7 8 9

Our Sunday Visitor Publishing Division
Our Sunday Visitor, Inc.
200 Noll Plaza
Huntington, IN 46750
www.osv.com
1-800-348-2440

ISBN: 978-1-63966-104-6 (Inventory No. T2831)
1. RELIGION—Holidays—Christmas & Advent.
2. RELIGION—Christian Living—Prayer.
3. RELIGION—Christianity—Catholic.
eISBN: 978-1-63966-105-3
LCCN: 2023936454

Cover design: Tyler Ottinger
Cover and Interior art: AdobeStock
Interior design: Amanda Falk

PRINTED IN THE UNITED STATES OF AMERICA

Dedicated to the Queen of Heaven
in gratitude for her visit to Champion, Wisconsin,
on October 9, 1859

+

To the seven pilgrims from the 2022 walking pilgrimage

+

And to my fellow Oriens *2022 pilgrims, especially*
those who joined me in the Virtual Bible study

+

¡Buen Camino!

WEEK 1
Sunday, December 3
ADVENT, 1ST SUNDAY

Wednesday, December 6 — ST. NICHOLAS

Friday, December 8 — IMMACULATE CONCEPTION

WEEK 2
Sunday, December 10
ADVENT, 2ND SUNDAY

Tuesday, December 12 — OUR LADY OF GUADALUPE

WEEK 3
Sunday, December 17
ADVENT, 3RD SUNDAY

WEEK 4
Sunday, December 24
ADVENT, 4TH SUNDAY

Monday, December 25 — NATIVITY OF OUR LORD

WEEK 5
Sunday, December 31
HOLY FAMILY

Monday, January 1 — MARY, MOTHER OF GOD

Saturday, January 6 — EPIPHANY

WEEK 6
Sunday, January 7
EPIPHANY, OBSERVED

Monday, January 8 — BAPTISM OF THE LORD

WEEK 7
Sunday, January 14
ORDINARY TIME, 2ND SUNDAY

WEEK 8
Sunday, January 21
ORDINARY TIME, 3RD SUNDAY

WEEK 9
Sunday, January 28
ORDINARY TIME, 4TH SUNDAY

Friday, February 2 — THE PRESENTATION OF THE LORD

Contents

Introduction

Give a man a fish, you feed him for a day.
Teach a man to pray and you feed him for a lifetime.

TEACH A MAN TO PRAY …

There are many wonderful Advent books full of moving meditations for you to choose from. This isn't one of them. Instead of giving you meditations I came up with, *Oriens* will teach you how to meditate for yourself. If you don't really know how to pray with Scripture, this book will teach you. If you already know how to pray, then it will help you to pray better. I left space each day for you to journal your prayer experiences. When you get to the end of the book, you will find it has become full of moving meditations, but they won't be my meditations; they'll be yours. I hope that, as you learn to go deeper in your conversations with God, prayer becomes your favorite part of each day, and this season takes on a whole new meaning.

IF YOU HAVE PRAYED WITH *ORIENS* BEFORE

You might be wondering how this book compares to previous editions. The format is exactly the same: We teach *lectio divina* and imaginative prayer, provide a Scripture passage each day, and give you space to journal. You will encounter familiar figures like John the Baptist, Zechariah, and, of course, Mary and Joseph. *Oriens* 2023 will be like walking down a familiar road, but with new companions and at a new place in your life. If you've never done *Oriens* before, finish reading the Introduction and then skim the rest of the introductory material through the first day (Sunday, December 3). That will give you a good sense of the road ahead.

"DO YOU WANT TO WALK THE *CAMINO* WITH ME?"

It was my third year of Theology at the Pontifical North American College in Rome. We had two weeks of Easter vacation to go experience Europe. A classmate and I decided to walk the *Camino Portugués*, a shorter version of the famous medieval pilgrimage route across Spain. (It's so famous that it's called *El Camino*, which simply means "the way" in Spanish.) I bought some shoes and borrowed a backpack, and we flew to Lisbon. We took a train to the Portuguese border and spent a week walking to the burial place of St. James the Apostle. Something special happened on the way. I started to see myself, and the ordinary world, in a whole new way. And I fell in love with walking pilgrimages.

Three years later I was back in America as a newly ordained priest. "We don't have to fly to Europe to walk down the road," I thought. I scoped out a walking route to a local shrine, lined up places to stay every twelve miles or so, and found people to bring us food each night. Twenty-two people joined me on the pilgrimage. Their lives were changed, and I became hooked on pilgrimages. Every year for the past ten years, I've led a five-day walking pilgrimage to the Shrine of Our Lady of Good Help in Champion, Wisconsin. I never cease to come away with some new gift, blessing, or lesson learned on the way.

Walking pilgrimages are much different experiences from bus pilgrimages. When you ride a bus to a shrine, it's mostly about the destination. Pilgrims look forward to a big "Aha" moment waiting for them when they arrive. Walking pilgrims, on the other hand, learn the joy of the journey. They see familiar roads in a whole new way. They appreciate the beauty around them. They enter into the ebb and flow of nature. They draw closer to the people they walk with. They learn to keep their eyes open for encounters with God along the way. Most of all, they learn to put one foot in front of the other and keep walking no matter what.

A walking pilgrimage is about more than the destination; it's a journey of the heart. It changes you in ways you never expected.

THE ADVENT JOURNEY

So what does this have to do with Advent? We all struggle with Advent. The Church is telling us to slow down, but the world is telling us, "Hurry up." We rush around preparing for the birth of Jesus. We look forward to the big "Aha" moment waiting for us at Christmas. And we always seem to miss out somehow. How is it that every year Christmas seems less merry and bright than we were hoping it would be?

The problem is that we keep treating Advent like the busy bus on the way to Christmas. We expect to step off at Bethlehem and have some kind of amazing experience. Yet Holy Mother Church designed Advent to be more like a walking pilgrimage. You take a little step every day. If you're open to it, you learn to enjoy the journey. You connect with the people around you. You enter into a new rhythm. The ordinary things of life start to take on a new meaning. God meets you on the road.

Think of this book as a *Camino* guidebook. It will show you how to step off the Christmas bus and walk the Advent road one day at a time. You will learn that Advent and Christmas are more than destinations; they involve a journey of the heart.

KEEP WALKING

This book covers nearly ten weeks, from the first Sunday of Advent on December 3 to the feast of the Presentation on February 2. Why does it go so long? This book is set up to let us spend four weeks preparing and forty days celebrating Christmas (kind of like the forty days of Lent followed by the fifty days of Easter).

We need those extra days. None of the people who saw the Christ Child in person understood the true meaning of Christmas. It was only in the days and years afterward that the "daybreak from on high" began to rise in their hearts (see Lk 1:78). The same is true for us in our ongoing journey of faith. Keeping this devotional until February 2 will help you continue to see Jesus in the ordinary. Besides, it's easier to pray in the post-Christmas lull, and we need a little help getting through the low time in January.

You don't have to walk the whole way with me; it's your journey and you can quit any time. But let me encourage you to plan for a longer walk. Consider putting up your Christmas tree a little later this year. Put on the lights and ornaments but don't plug in the lights until Light of the World is born on December 25. Then keep your tree lit all through the twelve days until January 6. Plan to keep at least your Advent wreath and Nativity scene up until February 2, the feast of the Presentation (also known as Candlemas). It may seem like a long way to go now, but you'll be surprised at how quickly it passes. And you'll really enjoy those extra days.

IF YOU MISS A DAY

Even when you are too busy to pray, try to at least open this book and read the Scripture passage each day. If you end up missing a day or two (or even a week), don't try to go back and do all the meditations you missed. Just skip ahead to the current day and pray that one well. It is not important that you do every single meditation. What matters is that you put your heart into your prayer. Prayer is experiencing how our Father looks at you with love. Holiness is learning to live in his long, loving gaze every moment of your life.

NO ONE WALKS ALONE

You might assume because I wrote this book that I'm great at praying. Far from it! I was trained as a spiritual director through the Institute for Priestly Formation. I have taught countless numbers of people how to pray. I've been on pilgrimages and retreats and even a thirty-day silent retreat. But the truth is, unless I'm actually on a retreat or a pilgrimage, I usually pray badly. Most days I'm too busy, distracted, self-absorbed, or lazy to really pray well. And the problem is compounded during the busy Advent and Christmas season. I wrote this book because I need it, too! I will be praying with you and for you this whole season. Please pray for me and for your fellow *Oriens* pilgrims. Consider joining me for a virtual Bible study each week. We will meet on Zoom to share our stories of the journey and encourage one another. Visit https://pilgrimpriest.us/book to learn more and sign up for free. We each make our own journey, and every journey is unique, but no one walks alone. *¡Buen Camino!*

Fr. Joel Sember
Priest, Pastor, Pilgrim

Suggested Calendar for the Advent and Christmas Season

December 3, First Sunday of Advent: Light the first candle on your Advent wreath.

December 6 (Wednesday): Give some treats for Saint Nicholas Day.

December 8 (Friday): Solemnity of the Immaculate Conception. Put up your crèche (manger scene).

December 10, Second Sunday of Advent: Light the second candle on your Advent wreath.

December 17, Third Sunday of Advent: Light the third (rose) candle on your Advent wreath.

Before December 24: Put up your Christmas tree. Decorate it, but don't plug the lights in. Wait until the Light of the World is born.

December 24, Fourth Sunday of Advent: Light the fourth candle on your Advent wreath.

December 24 or 25: After attending Christmas Mass, put the Baby Jesus in the crèche and light up your Christmas tree. Change the candles in your Advent wreath to white.

January 1 (Monday), Octave Day of Christmas, Solemnity of Mary the Mother of God: Start the New Year with Mary.

January 6 (Saturday), Epiphany: Have a family party to bless your home with blessed chalk. Afterward you can take down the tree (if you want to) and the decorations, but don't take down the Advent wreath or the crèche.

February 2 (Friday), Feast of the Presentation: Have one last Christmas party! Light the candles on your wreath and have a family Candlemas procession to the crèche. Sing Christmas carols. Then put away any remaining Christmas decorations.

Blessing of an Advent Wreath

The use of the Advent wreath is a traditional practice that has found its place in the Church as well as in the home. The blessing of an Advent wreath takes place on the First Sunday of Advent or on the evening before the First Sunday of Advent. When the blessing of the Advent wreath is celebrated in the home, it is appropriate that it be blessed by a parent or another member of the family.

All make the sign of the cross together: + In the Name of the Father, and of the Son, and of the Holy Spirit.
Leader: Our help is in the name of the Lord.
Response: Who made heaven and earth.
A reading from the book of the prophet Isaiah:

> *The people who walked in darkness*
> *have seen a great light;*
> *Upon those who dwelt in the land of gloom*
> *a light has shone.*
> *You have brought them abundant joy*
> *and great rejoicing;*
> *As they rejoice before you as at the harvest,*
> *as men make merry when dividing spoils. ...*
> *For a child is born to us, a son is given us;*
> *upon his shoulder dominion rests.*
> *They name him Wonder-Counselor, God-Hero,*
> *Father-Forever, Prince of Peace.*
> *His dominion is vast*
> *and forever peaceful,*
> *From David's throne, and over his kingdom,*
> *which he confirms and sustains.*
> *By judgment and justice,*
> *both now and forever. (Is 9:1–2, 5–6)*

Leader: The Word of the Lord.
Response: Thanks be to God.

Leader: Let us pray.

> Lord our God, we praise you for your Son, Jesus Christ: He is Emmanuel, the hope of the peoples, he is the wisdom that teaches and guides us, he is the Savior of every nation.
>
> Lord God, let your blessing come upon us as we light the candles of this wreath. May the wreath and its light be a sign of Christ's promise to bring us salvation. May he come quickly and not delay. We ask this through Christ our Lord.

Response: Amen.

The blessing may conclude with a verse from "O Come, O Come, Emmanuel":

> O come, desire of nations, bind
> in one the hearts of humankind
> bid ev'ry sad division cease
> and be thyself our Prince of peace.
> Rejoice! Rejoice! Emmanuel
> shall come to thee, O Israel.

— From *Catholic Household Blessings & Prayers*

Week One

Lectio Divina

This first week we will use an ancient prayer form called *lectio divina* (pronounced "LEK-si-o di-VEE-na"). It has four simple steps, known by their Latin names: *lectio* (reading), *meditatio* (meditation), *oratio* (prayer), and *contemplatio* (contemplation). Don't worry about each Latin word. The prayer form is as simple as this: read, think, talk, listen.

We read a passage of Scripture and lots of thoughts come to our mind: What does this word mean? What is the cultural and historical context? How have scholars interpreted this particular idea? Those aren't bad things to research. Some of those questions can form the *meditatio* part of the prayer. But we need to avoid getting stuck in our own heads.

Reading Scripture isn't really prayer if it doesn't turn into a conversation. That is why we read, think about what we have read, and then talk to God about what we are thinking. The fourth step is to listen, so it won't be a one-sided conversation. Many people find the *contemplatio* to be a difficult step; they worry about if they are "doing it right" or "if it's really God." Don't try too hard. Just be quiet and receive for a little while.

Prayer is not so much about getting something from God as it is about just being with God. We are using Scripture as a conversation starter, but conversations with God go deeper than words. Don't worry, I'll walk you through it.

Grace of the Week: Each week has a particular theme or focus. The first week will focus on the creation of the world, the plants, the animals, and human beings. The simplest things can be the easiest to forget, and the most profound when they are rediscovered. Pray for the grace to wonder anew at the marvel, mystery, and miracle of God's creation.

December 3 — Sunday

First Sunday of Advent

Preparation: Take a deep breath or two. Name three to five things you are grateful for. Say a prayer of thanksgiving to God for his blessings in your life.

***Lectio*:** Today we begin our Advent journey. Let's take a moment to plan the trip. Take a look at the calendar and make some notes about how you can really enjoy Advent and Christmas this year.

You have twenty-two days until Christmas. But Christmas is not the only stop on our journey. We will stop to enjoy St. Nicholas Day this Wednesday. Immaculate Conception is a holy day of obligation, so plan to attend Mass this coming Friday, December 8. When will you put up your Christmas tree? Try to make it a family event. Whenever you put up your Christmas tree, I encourage you not to light it until after Christmas Mass. When will you put out your Christmas crèche? Take some time to plan these activities in advance.

For now, the only thing you need to do is put out the Advent wreath and light the first candle. Everything else can happen in time. While you're looking at your calendar, you might want to plan a little time for baking, sending cards, present-wrapping, and quality family time — whatever makes Christmas special for you.

You might be feeling just a little anxious now that I brought up all those tasks. It's normal to be anxious during Advent and Christmas. But this year we're not just going to plan Advent, we are also going to pray with Advent. What are God's plans for your Advent season? Read the Scripture passage slowly and prayerfully.

MARK 13:33–37 (LECTIONARY)

Jesus said to his disciples: "Be watchful! Be alert! You do not know when the time will come. It is like a man traveling abroad. He leaves home and places his servants in charge, each with his work, and orders the gatekeeper to be on the watch. Watch, therefore; you do not know when

> *the lord of the house is coming, whether in the evening, or at midnight, or at cockcrow, or in the morning. May he not come suddenly and find you sleeping. What I say to you, I say to all: 'Watch!'"*

***Meditatio*:** The Latin word for watch is *vigilate*. Soldiers divided the night into four "watches" during which they would take turns staying up and keeping lookout for trouble. When Jesus calls us to "watch," then, he means staying awake ("keeping vigil") and also keeping watch (being "vigilant"). Soldiers would decide in advance who would be up for each of the four watches and what would be the best location to keep a lookout. We should also take some time here at the beginning to answer those same questions: *when* and *where*.

When will you pray? I like to pray right when I get up in the morning. Some people like to pray in the quiet of the evening. It may not happen exactly as you planned every day, but if you don't plan it, chances are it won't happen. Plan a time for prayer.

Where will you pray? If you don't already have a prayer room or a prayer corner, make one. It should be free of distractions and full of things that help you focus on God. Plan a place for prayer.

Now, read the passage a second time.

***Oratio*:** Let's not just plan for a good Advent, let's also pray about it. You can be sure that God has a plan for your Advent and Christmas. Are we focused on making our plan work, or are we open to accepting God's plan, whatever it might be? The watch we are called to keep is not a physical sleeplessness but rather a spiritual openness. Open your heart to God's plan. Pray, "Come, Holy Spirit, enlighten the eyes of my heart" (see Eph 1:18).

What do you want to get out of this season? What do you most deeply desire? What do you fear? As you reflect on these questions, turn to God in your heart. Speak to him the thoughts, feelings, and desires of your heart.

***Contemplatio*:** Read the passage a third time.

Now just try to receive whatever it is that God wants to give you.

Don't try too hard to receive. Just be open to whatever feeling, image, thought, or idea might rise to the surface of your mind. Feelings of peace, comfort, or clarity often accompany the presence of God. The point of this last step is not so much to get something from God but rather to be with the God who loves you and will be with you through Advent and Christmas. Just be with the Lord for a couple minutes before looking at the questions below.

SUGGESTIONS FOR JOURNALING

After each prayer time I will offer a few questions. This is not a test or quiz. The questions are provided to help you sift through your prayer time. You may have already had a wonderful prayer time and have no need of these questions. Other times you might find that nothing seems to have "happened" in your prayer time, and the questions might tease out something of the gift or blessing you received. Use whatever you find helpful and skip the rest.

1. What makes me excited for this prayer pilgrimage is …
2. I'm nervous about …
3. My favorite thing about Christmas last year was …
4. My place for prayer will be …
5. My time for prayer will be …
6. What I really want for Christmas is …
7. As a result of my prayer time, I feel that …

The most important part of our Advent journey is an attitude of thanksgiving. So thank God for today's prayer time and close with an Our Father.

December 4 — Monday

Monday of the First Week of Advent

Preparation: *Come, Holy Spirit, enlighten the eyes of my heart* (see Eph 1:18).

***Lectio*:** Ask God for the grace to wonder anew at the marvel, mystery, and miracle of his creation. This story of creation has been with the human race for a very, very long time. Read the passage slowly and prayerfully. As you do, picture a wizened elder telling the story to his grandchildren while they sit around a campfire in the darkness. There is no light pollution. Above their heads wave the ghostly shadows of trees, and above that stretches the vast carpet of stars. Beyond the flickering reaches of the campfire's warm light, they are wrapped in dense darkness. The children lean in to hear the story for the hundredth time.

GENESIS 1:1–5, 14–19

In the beginning, when God created the heavens and the earth — and the earth was without form or shape, with darkness over the abyss and a mighty wind sweeping over the waters —

Then God said: Let there be light, and there was light. God saw that the light was good. God then separated the light from the darkness. God called the light "day," and the darkness he called "night." Evening came, and morning followed — the first day....

Then God said: Let there be lights in the dome of the sky, to separate day from night. Let them mark the seasons, the days and the years, and serve as lights in the dome of the sky, to illuminate the earth. And so it happened: God made the two great lights, the greater one to govern the day, and the lesser one to govern the night, and the stars. God set them in the dome of the sky, to illuminate the earth, to govern the day and the night, and to separate the light from the darkness. God saw that it was good. Evening came, and morning followed — the fourth day.

***Meditatio*:** We begin *in the beginning* with the creation of the world. The Bible starts by explaining that everything that is comes from God. The details are not as important as the feeling. Try to get a sense of the majesty and mystery of it all — recall the ancient patriarch telling this story to his grandchildren around a campfire.

The Bible opens to a scene of a wind-swept sea in total darkness. The Hebrew word for wind also means "spirit" and "breath." The wind is the "spirit" or "breath" of God.

God is here, and he breaks the silence with four simple words: "Let there be light." And so it is. God's word becomes physical in the sun, which gives light and life, and in the moon and stars, which light the night. They are visible signs that point to the Creator. What do they say about God? Read the passage again.

***Oratio*:** The word *oriens* comes from a Latin verb that means "rising," "dawn," and "East." It is pronounced *OR-ee-ens*, with the accent on the first syllable like the English words "Orient" and Oreo cookie, and gives us the English words "Oriental" and "orientation." We find it in the Canticle of Zechariah: "Because of the tender mercy of our God by which the daybreak from on high will visit us" (Lk 1:78). *Oriens* can also mean "rising one," perhaps a veiled reference to Jesus' resurrection.

One of the rich symbols of Advent is the light overcoming the darkness. More than just physical light, our hearts long for spiritual light. Even if prayer feels dark, we know that we are not alone. The Spirit of God is moving here.

Break the silence and speak to your Maker. What do you want to say to God?

***Contemplatio*:** Open your heart to receive whatever God might want to give you. How is God's light shining on you?

Read the passage very slowly a third time. Don't sweat this step. Think of it like sensing the direction of the wind or basking for a moment in the sun's light. Contemplation is being in relationship. Just be with the God who is always with you, and receive his loving presence.

SUGGESTIONS FOR JOURNALING

1. What stood out to me this time as I read the Creation story?
2. What was my most noticeable thought, feeling, or desire during prayer time today?
3. Did I notice God's presence in any particular way? If I did, how would I describe it? If not, how did I feel about it?
4. Can I name one area in my life where I want God's light to shine a little more brightly this Advent?

After you've journaled, close with a brief conversation giving thanks to God for your prayer today. Then pray an Our Father.

December 5 — Tuesday

Tuesday of the First Week of Advent

Preparation: *Come, Holy Spirit, enlighten the eyes of my heart.* Spend a minute or so reflecting on the beauty of the world that surrounds us. Let your heart be grateful for God's creation.

***Lectio*:** Ask God for the grace to wonder anew at the marvel, mystery, and miracle of his creation. Read the passage slowly and prayerfully.

PSALM 104:1–18

Bless the Lord, my soul!
Lord, my God, you are great indeed!
You are clothed with majesty and splendor,
robed in light as with a cloak.
You spread out the heavens like a tent;
setting the beams of your chambers upon the waters.
You make the clouds your chariot;
traveling on the wings of the wind.
You make the winds your messengers;
flaming fire, your ministers.

You fixed the earth on its foundation,
so it can never be shaken.
The deeps covered it like a garment;
above the mountains stood the waters.
At your rebuke they took flight;
at the sound of your thunder they fled.
They rushed up the mountains, down the valleys
to the place you had fixed for them.
You set a limit they cannot pass;
never again will they cover the earth.

You made springs flow in wadies
that wind among the mountains.
They give drink to every beast of the field;
here wild asses quench their thirst.
Beside them the birds of heaven nest;
among the branches they sing.
You water the mountains from your chambers;
from the fruit of your labor the earth abounds.
You make the grass grow for the cattle
and plants for people's work
to bring forth food from the earth,
wine to gladden their hearts,
oil to make their faces shine,
and bread to sustain the human heart.
The trees of the Lord drink their fill,
the cedars of Lebanon, which you planted.
There the birds build their nests;
the stork in the junipers, its home.
The high mountains are for wild goats;
the rocky cliffs, a refuge for badgers.

***Meditatio*:** The heavens are always above us, yet we rarely notice them. The times and seasons all speak to us of God's providence. For modern Americans, nature is just the scenery that flashes by on our drive to work or Walmart. Many of us, hopefully, had a chance to "get out in nature" over the summer.

Recall a time when you marveled at God's handiwork, when his creation really spoke to you. What was it saying? How did you feel?

***Oratio*:** God is both engineer and artist. Read the passage again slowly. Notice the word or phrase that most speaks to you or the image that moves your heart. When you are done reading the passage, talk to God about it. Say to him whatever has come to your mind.

***Contemplatio*:** Skim the passage, pausing on the place that most spoke to you or touched you. Open your heart, and let your Creator speak to you. Receive whatever it is that God wants to give you. He cares for all his creation, but he cares especially for you. Rest quietly for a moment or two in his loving presence.

SUGGESTIONS FOR JOURNALING

1. How do the heavens look different if I see them as a fruit of God's handiwork instead of just a vast "space"?
2. How do the creatures around me testify to God's goodness?
3. The ancients saw all of creation as a cosmic symphony singing God's praises. What part of the symphony most speaks to me?
4. What does it say about God's glory?
5. I needed to tell God that ...
6. I sensed God saying to me ...
7. I left prayer wanting ...

After you've journaled, close with a brief conversation giving thanks to God for your prayer today. Then pray an Our Father.

December 6 — Wednesday

Wednesday of the First Week of Advent

SAINT NICHOLAS, BISHOP

Saint Nicholas was the bishop of Myra in modern-day Turkey. He died on this day around AD 350. He is one of the most popular Christian saints, though very little is known about him. He is a patron of mariners, merchants, bakers, travelers, and children. There are many legends associated with him, one of which is that he brings little gifts to children on his feast day.

Preparation: *Come, Holy Spirit, enlighten the eyes of my heart.* Spend a minute or so reflecting on the world that surrounds us. Let your heart be grateful for God's creation.

***Lectio*:** Ask God for the grace to wonder anew at the marvel, mystery, and miracle of his creation. Read the passage slowly and prayerfully. God not only created the world, but also governs it. The sun shines on all creation, sees all things, and provides warmth and light to all things. In a similar way, God looks down from the heavens and sees and hears everything. He governs all things, providing commands that guide us wisely.

PSALM 104:19–35

You made the moon to mark the seasons,
the sun that knows the hour of its setting.
You bring darkness and night falls,
then all the animals of the forest wander about.
Young lions roar for prey;
they seek their food from God.
When the sun rises, they steal away
and settle down in their dens.
People go out to their work,
to their labor till evening falls.

How varied are your works, LORD!
In wisdom you have made them all;
the earth is full of your creatures.
There is the sea, great and wide!
It teems with countless beings,
living things both large and small.
There ships ply their course
and Leviathan, whom you formed to play with.

All of these look to you
to give them food in due time.
When you give it to them, they gather;
when you open your hand, they are well filled.
When you hide your face, they panic.
Take away their breath, they perish
and return to the dust.
Send forth your spirit, they are created
and you renew the face of the earth.

May the glory of the LORD endure forever;
may the LORD be glad in his works!
Who looks at the earth and it trembles,
touches the mountains and they smoke!
I will sing to the LORD all my life;
I will sing praise to my God while I live.
May my meditation be pleasing to him;
I will rejoice in the LORD.
May sinners vanish from the earth,
and the wicked be no more.
Bless the LORD, my soul! Hallelujah!

***Meditatio*:** The Hebrew word for spirit, *ruach* (roo-ak), also means breath or wind. The Bible thinks of the life breath that all living things have, their "spirit," as coming from God. When God takes this gift back, living things perish, and as they decompose, they become a source of new life.

God's *ruach* is the force that animates and renews. Read the passage again slowly. Notice what part speaks to you personally.

***Oratio*:** God orders all the things around you, but he also provides food and other life-giving support for you personally. Speak to God. Ask him to breathe his spirit on you and renew your life. When you are done speaking, read the passage one more time, or just the part that most speaks to you.

***Contemplatio*:** Open your heart to receive what God wants to say to you. Maybe it is a thought, a word, or a sense of peace. Maybe you just feel more grateful. Or perhaps you feel his spirit moving in a new and powerful way. Spend a moment being in the presence of God and just receiving his loving care.

SUGGESTIONS FOR JOURNALING

1. The part of this passage that most spoke to me was …
2. I felt the Spirit of God moving when …
3. My strongest thought, feeling, or desire during prayer was …
4. I sensed God communicating to me …
5. I ended prayer wanting …

After you've journaled, close with a brief conversation giving thanks to God for your prayer experience. Then pray an Our Father.

December 7 — Thursday

Thursday of the First Week of Advent

Preparation: *Come, Holy Spirit, enlighten the eyes of my heart.* Spend a minute or so reflecting on the world that surrounds us. Let your heart be grateful for God's creation.

***Lectio*:** Ask God for the grace to wonder anew at the marvel, mystery, and miracle of his creation.

Job has been struck with terrible misfortune. His friends have come to visit him. They tell him he must have done something to deserve his misfortune. Job responds to each friend to declare his innocence and demand that God answer for his unjust actions. Finally, in a great biblical *Deus ex machina*, God himself begins to speak.

Read the passage slowly and prayerfully.

JOB 38:1–21

Then the Lord answered Job out of the storm and said:
Who is this who darkens counsel
with words of ignorance?
Gird up your loins now, like a man;
I will question you, and you tell me the answers!
Where were you when I founded the earth?
Tell me, if you have understanding.
Who determined its size? Surely you know?
Who stretched out the measuring line for it?
Into what were its pedestals sunk,
and who laid its cornerstone,
While the morning stars sang together
and all the sons of God shouted for joy?
Who shut within doors the sea,
when it burst forth from the womb,
When I made the clouds its garment

and thick darkness its swaddling bands?
When I set limits for it
and fastened the bar of its door,
And said: Thus far shall you come but no farther,
and here shall your proud waves stop?
Have you ever in your lifetime commanded the morning
and shown the dawn its place
For taking hold of the ends of the earth,
till the wicked are shaken from it?
The earth is changed as clay by the seal,
and dyed like a garment;
But from the wicked their light is withheld,
and the arm of pride is shattered.
Have you entered into the sources of the sea,
or walked about on the bottom of the deep?
Have the gates of death been shown to you,
or have you seen the gates of darkness?
Have you comprehended the breadth of the earth?
Tell me, if you know it all.
What is the way to the dwelling of light,
and darkness — where is its place?
That you may take it to its territory
and know the paths to its home?
You know, because you were born then,
and the number of your days is great!

***Meditatio*:** If these words were spoken to me from the midst of a storm cloud, I would feel very small and terrified. It might sound like God is rebuking Job. However, God never accuses Job of saying or doing anything wrong. He will, in fact, take Job's side against his friends (Job 42:7–8). Instead, God is responding to Job's attitude that the Creator must answer to his creature. When have we been guilty of the same attitude as Job? God speaks with sarcasm to a tiny creature whom he loves dearly.

Read the passage again slowly. This time notice the word or phrase that most speaks to you.

Oratio**:** Let's not just talk about God, but actually talk to God. Have there been times when you wanted God to explain himself to you? Speak from your heart. Do not be afraid of offending God.

When you are done speaking, review the part of the passage that most spoke to you.

Contemplatio**:** Open your heart to receive what God wants to say to you. Maybe it is a thought, a word, or a sense of peace. Perhaps it is a new perspective on the relationship between creature and creator. Spend a moment or two receiving.

SUGGESTIONS FOR JOURNALING

1. When I read this passage the first time, I felt …
2. The part of this passage that stood out to me was …
3. My strongest thought, feeling, or desire during prayer was …
4. I had a hard time with …
5. God wanted me to know that …

After you've journaled, close with a brief conversation giving thanks to God for your prayer experience. Then pray an Our Father.

December 8 — Friday

Solemnity of the Immaculate Conception

The Christian Church has long believed that the Blessed Virgin Mary was preserved free from all sin starting at the very moment of her conception. Christians have celebrated this feast for over 1,200 years, but it was officially declared a dogma by Pope Blessed Pius IX in 1854. Four years later, Our Lady appeared to Saint Bernadette at Lourdes, France, and told her, "I am the Immaculate Conception." Today's feast is a holy day of obligation for Catholics, and the Gloria is sung at Mass.

Preparation: *Come, Holy Spirit, enlighten the eyes of my heart.* Call to mind an experience of God's loving providence in your daily life. Let gratitude rise in your heart as you spend a minute resting in God's unconditional love for you.

***Lectio*:** Ask God for the grace to wonder anew at the marvel, mystery, and miracle of his creation.

Why are humans the only creatures that wear clothing? Today's passage addresses this question. Adam and Eve were created naked, but they didn't seem to notice and it didn't bother them. They had a kind of childlike innocence that was lost when they ate from the forbidden tree. Immediately, they felt shame and the desire to hide.

Read through this passage. Reflect on how each person (including God) might be feeling.

GENESIS 3:9–15, 20 (LECTIONARY)

After the man, Adam, had eaten of the tree, the LORD God then called to the man and asked him: "Where are you?" He answered, "I heard you in the garden; but I was afraid, because I was naked, so I hid myself." Then he asked: "Who told you that you were naked? You have eaten, then, from the tree of which I had forbidden you to eat!"

The man replied, "The woman whom you put here with me — she gave me fruit from the tree, so I ate it." The LORD God then asked the woman, Why did you do such a thing? The woman answered, "The serpent tricked me into it, so I ate it."

Then the LORD God said to the serpent:
"Because you have done this, you shall be banned
from all the animals
and from all the wild creatures;
on your belly shall you crawl,
and dirt you shall eat
all the days of your life.
I will put enmity between you and the woman,
and between your offspring and hers;
he will strike at your head,
while you strike at their heel." ...

The man called his wife Eve, because she became the mother of all the living.

Meditatio: God knows everything; he already knows what Adam and Eve have done. He is trying to coax his scared creatures back to a relationship with him, but they are too afraid. God then makes a prophecy that the woman's offspring will crush the serpent's head. Thousands of years later, Christians would recognize this as a reference to Jesus Christ. God has gone to great lengths to rescue us.

Read the passage a second time.

Oratio: When have you done wrong and felt ashamed? Do you feel unworthy of God's friendship? Do you try to keep a safe distance between you and God?

Picture God speaking to you directly. Try to be completely honest with God about what you have done and what it feels like to be in his presence.

Contemplatio: Read the passage a third time.

Open your heart to receive whatever God might want to say to you.

It may be just a simple, "I love you." You may sense a twinkle in his eye or a willingness to wait patiently until you are ready to be with him. Enjoy the presence of God for a minute or two before moving on.

SUGGESTIONS FOR JOURNALING

1. My strongest thought, feeling, or desire during prayer was …
2. A new insight I received was …
3. I experience shame when …
4. I sensed God communicating to me …
5. I ended prayer wanting …

After you've journaled, close with a brief conversation giving thanks to God for your prayer experience. Then pray an Our Father.

December 9 — Saturday

Saturday of the First Week of Advent

ST. JUAN DIEGO

On this day in 1532, a native Chichimeca man was on his way to Mass when he heard a voice calling his name. A beautiful woman was standing on the hill of Tepeyac near present-day Mexico City. She told him that she was the Virgin Mother of the true God. She wanted him to go speak to the bishop and ask for a church to be built on that hill so she could manifest her love for all people.

The bishop was skeptical and sent Juan Diego back to ask the lady for a sign. However, that night Juan Diego's uncle took sick. After he cared for his uncle until it seemed that the end was near, Juan Diego ran to get a priest for the Anointing of the Sick. He tried to avoid the lady by going the other way around the hill, but then he saw her coming down the hill to meet him. She told Juan Diego not to worry about his uncle, then sent him up the hill to pick some roses, which were blooming miraculously in the December cold. She arranged them with her own hands in his *tilma* (a kind of poncho made of cactus fiber) and then sent him to town saying he should show the sign to no one but the bishop himself.

REVIEW

Preparation: *Come, Holy Spirit, enlighten the eyes of my heart.* Spend a minute or so reflecting on your blessings. Let gratitude rise in your heart.

St. Ignatius of Loyola encouraged his retreat participants to make a repetition. This means that you circle back to the place where you most experienced God's love for you. Let's take some time to reflect on your time with God this week. Flip back through your past week's journal entries. Notice what emerged in the conversations. Here are some questions to help you:

1. My favorite time of prayer, or the one that most spoke to me,

was …

2. Where did I notice the presence and action of God?
3. What was he doing, saying, or giving me?
4. How did I respond to what God was doing?
5. I find myself struggling the most with …
6. I see prayer in a different light because …
7. I'm grateful for …

What is one image of God's loving presence that emerged from your prayer during this first week?

Savor that image of God's loving presence. Rest there for a minute or two. Then close with an Our Father.

Week Two

Imaginative Prayer

I hope you enjoyed *lectio divina*. This week we will learn a new prayer form called *imaginative prayer*. St. Ignatius of Loyola seems to have invented this prayer form while he was recuperating from battle wounds at his family's castle. He wanted to pass the time reading courtly romance novels but none could be found. All they had was a book on the lives of the saints and a book that retold the Gospels (like the Christian miniseries *The Chosen*). He began to read these books and imagine himself meeting Jesus in Bible times or living the life of a great saint. Other times he would think back to his favorite romance novels and imagine himself fighting great battles and winning the hand of a princess. His courtly daydreams left him feeling empty. However, his saintly daydreams gave him a sense of peace and joy that lasted. One day he noticed the difference and marveled at it. This simple insight was the beginning of his conversion.

Many people are skeptical of imaginative prayer. They wonder if they are inventing things and if God is really speaking to them through their prayer. Your imagination was created by God as a faculty of the intellect. It is a powerful tool and can be used to make Scripture come alive.

God is with you right now as you read these words. But you are more aware of your location in space and time, how you spent Saturday night, and what is coming up today. Through the imagination, we are able to step out of the here-and-now temporarily so as to access the deeper spiritual presence of God with us. The imagination becomes a springboard for an encounter with God.

Remember that prayer is really about spending time with the God who loves us. It's not about filling pages of a journal with amazing insights or experiences. If you are open to an encounter, then God will come and meet you. The imagination is only a conversation starter.

Grace of the Week: We are surrounded by God's creation. We are also creatures who were made by God for a relationship with him. This week we will explore our fall from a relationship with God and into the deep darkness of sin and death. Pray for the grace to experience how much pain this separation causes God, so as to experience a greater longing for relationship with him.

December 10 — Sunday
Second Sunday of Advent

Preparation: *Come, Holy Spirit, enlighten the eyes of my heart.* Flip back to that one image of God's loving presence that emerged in your prayer on Saturday. Spend about a minute resting there and living in that moment. Let gratitude rise in your heart.

Set the Scene: Ask God in your own words for the grace to experience how much pain our separation causes God, so you may experience a greater longing for relationship with him. The prophet Isaiah spoke these words to a people living in exile far from their homeland. The people had been invaded and conquered because they had not been faithful to God. God, however, has not abandoned his people. He himself will lead them home like a shepherd bringing his sheep in from the pasture. Read the passage and picture the scene in your mind.

ISAIAH 40:1–5, 9–11 (LECTIONARY)

Comfort, give comfort to my people, says your God.
Speak tenderly to Jerusalem, and proclaim to her that her service is at an end,
her guilt is expiated;
indeed, she has received from the hand of the LORD double for all her sins.
A voice cries out:
In the desert prepare the way of the LORD!
Make straight in the wasteland a highway for our God!
Every valley shall be filled in,
every mountain and hill shall be made low;
the rugged land shall be made a plain,
the rough country, a broad valley.
Then the glory of the LORD shall be revealed,
and all people shall see it together;
for the mouth of the LORD has spoken.
Go up onto a high mountain,

> *Zion, herald of glad tidings;*
> *cry out at the top of your voice,*
> *Jerusalem, herald of good news!*
> *Fear not to cry out*
> *and say to the cities of Judah:*
> *Here is your God!*
> *Here comes with power*
> *the Lord GOD,*
> *who rules by his strong arm;*
> *here is his reward with him,*
> *his recompense before him.*
> *Like a shepherd he feeds his flock;*
> *in his arms he gathers the lambs,*
> *carrying them in his bosom,*
> *and leading the ewes with care.*

Action! The glory of the Lord is revealed, and all the nations see it like a bright morning star. Can you place yourself in the scene? Perhaps picture yourself as a sheep in a herd far from home with no way to get back. Then God makes a smooth highway through the rough land and he himself walks this road to come get his sheep. He rounds them up and leads them home. Read the passage a second time.

Acknowledge: What did it feel like to be in exile? What did it feel like to be rescued? Name some of the words that come to mind. Notice your strongest thought, feeling, or desire.

Relate: Speak to the Shepherd about what is on your heart. Let him look at you with love. How does he respond?

Receive: Receive whatever is in God's heart for you — his thoughts, feelings, desires. This can be a difficult step for people. Don't try too hard. Read the passage a third time, or just the part that really speaks to you, and just be open to receive.

Respond: Whatever comes up, welcome it. Then try to respond to it. For example, you might notice the Shepherd's compassion and realize God has not abandoned his sheep. You respond by saying "Thank you" or by asking for help to not wander off again. Or you might feel like you are too weak to walk and you realize the Shepherd has picked you up and is carrying you. Respond with gratitude. Then just be with the Lord for a minute or two before moving on.

SUGGESTIONS FOR JOURNALING

1. My strongest thought, feeling, or desire was …
2. There was one particular fear that I noticed …
3. God was responding to me by …
4. I felt the love of God most strongly when …
5. The Shepherd is inviting me to …

After you've journaled, close with a brief conversation giving thanks to God for your prayer experience. You may be tempted to skip this, as you've already talked to God. Think of it like talking to a friend as you walk them out to their car after a nice visit. Thanks, God! Then pray one Our Father.

December 11 — Monday

Monday of the Second Week of Advent

Preparation: *Come, Holy Spirit, enlighten the eyes of my heart.* Recall an image of God's loving presence that has emerged in your prayer time so far. Spend a minute resting in the free, unearned gift of loving and being loved. Let gratitude rise in your heart.

Set the Scene: Ask God in your own words for the grace to experience how much pain our separation causes God, so as to experience a greater longing for relationship with him. Adam and Eve both ate from the Tree of the Knowledge of Good and Evil and were expelled from the garden. However, it didn't take long for their evil to grow into murder in the next generation. Sometimes artists show the smoke of Abel's sacrifice rising to heaven while the smoke from Cain's sacrifice stays heavy on the ground. Read through the passage once to picture the scene.

GENESIS 4:1–8

The man had intercourse with his wife Eve, and she conceived and gave birth to Cain, saying, "I have produced a male child with the help of the LORD." Next she gave birth to his brother Abel. Abel became a herder of flocks, and Cain a tiller of the ground.

In the course of time Cain brought an offering to the LORD from the fruit of the ground, while Abel, for his part, brought the fatty portion of the firstlings of his flock. The LORD looked with favor on Abel and his offering, but on Cain and his offering he did not look with favor. So Cain was very angry and dejected.

Then the LORD said to Cain: Why are you angry? Why are you dejected? If you act rightly, you will be accepted; but if not, sin lies in wait at the door: its urge is for you, yet you can rule over it.

> *Cain said to his brother Abel, "Let us go out in the field." When they were in the field, Cain attacked his brother Abel and killed him.*

Action! Read the passage again. This time let the scene play out in your mind. Rivalry between brothers is nothing new. In God's eyes, every murder is brother killing brother.

Acknowledge: Notice what is going on inside of you — your thoughts, feelings, and desires.

Relate: The same God who spoke to Cain is with you now. Turn to him and speak to him what is on your heart.

Receive: Your attention moves from your thoughts to God. What was God thinking and feeling in this moment? What is in God's heart for you right now? If you find yourself stuck, don't try too hard to "figure out" what God might be saying. Just shift your attention to God and see if there is a new awareness, insight, or understanding. Whatever it is, receive it. Read the passage a third time.

Respond: Receive what God has to give you, then answer him back again. Spend a few minutes in God's presence before you move on.

SUGGESTIONS FOR JOURNALING

1. What jumped out at me when I first read the passage was …
2. My strongest thought, feeling, or desire during prayer was …
3. I sensed God communicating to me …
4. I found the whole experience of prayer today to be …
5. I ended prayer wanting …

After you've journaled, close with a brief conversation giving thanks to God for your prayer experience. Then pray an Our Father.

December 12 — Tuesday

Tuesday of the Second Week of Advent

FEAST OF OUR LADY OF GUADALUPE

On December 12, 1532, Juan Diego arrived at the bishop's palace clutching something in his *tilma*. He refused to show it to anyone but the bishop. The bishop's servants made him wait for a long time before finally ushering him into the bishop's room. He unfolded his mantle, and Castilian roses tumbled out onto the floor. Even more surprisingly, a miraculous image of the lady who had appeared to him was imprinted on his *tilma*. The bishop and his entourage accompanied Juan Diego to check on his uncle, who turned out to be in perfect health after he, too, had a visit from the beautiful lady.

A shrine was built to house the miraculous *tilma*, and next to it a little house for Juan Diego. He spent the rest of his life telling his story as millions of native Aztecs converted to the Catholic Faith. The image hangs today in the shrine of Our Lady of Guadalupe on the outskirts of Mexico City. It testifies to her love for all people, including you.

Preparation: *Come, Holy Spirit, enlighten the eyes of my heart.* Recall an image of God's loving presence that has emerged in your prayer time so far. Spend about a minute resting in the free, unearned gift of loving and being loved. Let gratitude rise in your heart.

Set the Scene: Ask God in your own words for the grace to experience how much pain our separation causes God, so as to experience a greater longing for relationship with him. Yesterday's Scripture passage ended in a cliffhanger. Now we hear the rest of the story. Adam and Eve refused to admit they had done anything wrong when God found them hiding in the bushes (see Gn 3:11–14). Cain behaves in much the same way. Notice the emotions of the different actors as you read through the passage and picture the scene.

GENESIS 4:9–16

Then the LORD asked Cain, Where is your brother Abel? He answered, "I do not know. Am I my brother's keeper?" God then said: What have you done? Your brother's blood cries out to me from the ground! Now you are banned from the ground that opened its mouth to receive your brother's blood from your hand. If you till the ground, it shall no longer give you its produce. You shall become a constant wanderer on the earth.

Cain said to the LORD: "My punishment is too great to bear. Look, you have now banished me from the ground. I must avoid you and be a constant wanderer on the earth. Anyone may kill me at sight."

Not so! the LORD said to him. If anyone kills Cain, Cain shall be avenged seven times. So the LORD put a mark on Cain, so that no one would kill him at sight.

Cain then left the LORD's presence and settled in the land of Nod, east of Eden.

Action! Read the passage again. This time note the feelings of the different actors in the scene. Also notice where it doesn't play out exactly how you might have expected.

Acknowledge: Pay attention to what is going on inside of you—your thoughts, feelings, and desires.

Relate: Was God unfair in some way? Turn to him now and tell him what is on your heart.

Receive: Your attention moves from your thoughts to God. What was God thinking and feeling when he confronted Cain? What is in God's heart for you right now? Receive it. Read the passage a third time.

Respond: Respond to whatever God seems to be saying to you, even if it's only a thought, feeling, or insight. Spend a few minutes with the God who loves you before moving on.

SUGGESTIONS FOR JOURNALING

1. What jumped out at me when I first read the passage was …
2. My strongest thought, feeling, or desire during prayer was …
3. I sensed God communicating to me …
4. I found the whole experience of prayer today to be …
5. I ended prayer wanting …

After you've journaled, close with a brief conversation giving thanks to God for your prayer experience. Then pray an Our Father.

December 13 — Wednesday

Wednesday of the Second Week of Advent

SAINT LUCY, MARTYR

Little is known about this young Christian girl from Syracuse in Sicily. It is said that a disappointed suitor denounced her as a Christian and she was executed in AD 304. She is one of the seven women mentioned by name in the Roman Canon of the Mass (Eucharistic Prayer I).

Her name comes from the Latin word *lux* meaning "light." Because of this, she is the patroness of eyesight. Her feast day is celebrated with the lighting of candles and special foods, particularly in Scandinavian countries. Through the intercession of Saint Lucy, pray that God will enlighten your heart so as to make you a light for others.

Preparation: *Come, Holy Spirit, enlighten the eyes of my heart.* Call to mind an image of God's loving presence that you have experienced. Spend a minute resting in God's merciful love for you. Let gratitude rise in your heart.

Set the Scene: Ask God in your own words for the grace to experience how much pain our separation causes God, so as to experience a greater longing for relationship with him.

Today's reading is full of images. Read through the passage and imagine each part of the story: people walking around in darkness and living in a land of gloom. Suddenly, a bright light enlightens their world. Harvesters bring in an abundant crop. Slaves or the victims of war suddenly free, their shackles broken beyond repair, the tools of oppression now feeding a bonfire of celebration. Let your imagination run wild.

ISAIAH 9:1–6

The people who walked in darkness
have seen a great light;
Upon those who lived in the land of gloom

a light has shone.
You have brought them abundant joy
and great rejoicing;
They rejoice before you as people rejoice at harvest,
as they exult when dividing the spoils.
For the yoke that burdened them,
the pole on their shoulder,
The rod of their taskmaster
you have smashed, as on the day of Midian.
For every boot that tramped in battle,
every cloak rolled in blood,
will be burned as fuel for fire.
For a child is born to us, a son is given to us;
upon his shoulder dominion rests.
They name him Wonder-Counselor, God-Hero,
Father-Forever, Prince of Peace.
His dominion is vast
and forever peaceful,
Upon David's throne, and over his kingdom,
which he confirms and sustains
By judgment and justice,
both now and forever.
The zeal of the LORD of hosts will do this!

Action! What stood out to you? You don't have to picture every image, just let your imagination capture the movement from darkness to light, oppression to freedom, violence to peace.

Read the passage a second time. This time notice the feelings of the participants. Do these feelings connect with any experiences you have had? Set yourself in the scene.

Acknowledge: What word or phrase speaks to you most strongly? What is your strongest thought, feeling, or desire?

Relate: Picture the Lord of hosts in his zeal for his people sending them a hero, a child who is born to rule with judgment and justice a dominion that is vast and forever peaceful. Speak to him in your heart and share with him what stirred in you during the Acknowledge part of the prayer.

Receive: Open your heart to receive whatever God wants to give you. Perhaps you sense that he loves you and is with you, or that he hears and understands. Just be open to receive, without fear or expectation.

Read the passage a third time.

Respond: After receiving what God has to give you, answer him back again. It may be just a simple, "Thank you." Or it may be moving to deeper conversation. Just be with the Lord for a minute or two before moving on.

SUGGESTIONS FOR JOURNALING

1. The part of this passage that most spoke to me was …
2. My strongest thought, feeling, or desire was …
3. The burden I felt lifted was …
4. God was with me and wanted me to know …
5. A new insight or understanding I received was …

After you've journaled, close with a brief conversation giving thanks to God for your prayer experience. Then pray an Our Father.

December 14 — Thursday

Thursday of the Second Week of Advent

Preparation: *Come, Holy Spirit, enlighten the eyes of my heart.* Remind your heart of God's loving presence and spend the first minute of your prayer resting in the free, unearned gift of loving and being loved. Let gratitude rise in your heart.

Set the Scene: Ask God in your own words for the grace to experience how much pain our separation causes God, so as to experience a greater longing for relationship with him.

Read the passage. As you do, set the scene in your mind. Picture the scattered sheep on the hillsides, far from their own country.

EZEKIEL 34:11–15

> *For thus says the Lord GOD: Look! I myself will search for my sheep and examine them. As a shepherd examines his flock while he himself is among his scattered sheep, so will I examine my sheep. I will deliver them from every place where they were scattered on the day of dark clouds. I will lead them out from among the peoples and gather them from the lands; I will bring them back to their own country and pasture them upon the mountains of Israel, in the ravines and every inhabited place in the land. In good pastures I will pasture them; on the mountain heights of Israel will be their grazing land. There they will lie down on good grazing ground; in rich pastures they will be pastured on the mountains of Israel. I myself will pasture my sheep; I myself will give them rest — oracle of the Lord GOD.*

Action! Place yourself in the scene. What does it feel like to be scattered when it is cloudy and dark? What does it feel like to lie down on good grazing ground? In what way do you desire rest this Advent season?

Read the passage a second time.

Acknowledge: Is there a word, phrase, or image that stands out to you? Are you patiently trusting in God to rescue you, or do you find yourself tempted to self-pity or despair? Notice your strongest thought, feeling, or desire.

Relate: Speak to the Shepherd about what is on your heart. Let him look at you with love. Be completely honest with him; he already knows how you are feeling.

Receive: What is going on in God's heart as he gazes at the scene? How does he respond to what you have shared with him? Receive whatever is in God's heart for you — his thoughts, feelings, or desires.

Read the passage a third time as you focus on the Shepherd's heart.

Respond: Now answer him back again. Just be with the Shepherd for a minute or two before moving on.

SUGGESTIONS FOR JOURNALING

1. More than anything, my heart desires …
2. My greatest fear or struggle seems to be …
3. I sensed God communicating to me …
4. Today I sensed the Shepherd inviting me to …
5. I ended prayer with a greater sense …

After you've journaled, close with a brief conversation giving thanks to God for your prayer experience. Then pray an Our Father.

December 15 — Friday

Friday of the Second Week of Advent

Preparation: *Come, Holy Spirit, enlighten the eyes of my heart.* Call to mind God's loving presence and spend the first minute of your prayer resting in the free, unearned gift of loving and being loved. Let gratitude rise in your heart.

Set the Scene: Ask God in your own words for the grace to experience how much pain our separation causes God, so as to desire more deeply a relationship with him.

Read the passage. Think of green pastures and still waters, a picnic meal, and an afternoon nap in a field.

PSALM 23

The LORD is my shepherd;
there is nothing I lack.
In green pastures he makes me lie down;
to still waters he leads me;
he restores my soul.
He guides me along right paths
for the sake of his name.
Even though I walk through the valley of the shadow of death,
I will fear no evil, for you are with me;
your rod and your staff comfort me.

You set a table before me
in front of my enemies;
You anoint my head with oil;
my cup overflows.
Indeed, goodness and mercy will pursue me
all the days of my life;

I will dwell in the house of the LORD
for endless days.

Action! This passage contains the movements of the Paschal Triduum (Holy Thursday, Good Friday, Easter Sunday). First there is a peaceful time together with the Shepherd. Then there is a Good Friday moment of walking through the valley of the shadow of death, but without fear because the Shepherd walks with you. Finally, there is the banquet of heaven, a meal prepared for you in God's own house, and you never have to leave.

Read the passage a second time. This time picture it as an analogy for our lives.

Acknowledge: What do you feel as you put your own life into this psalm: Do you notice God's protective care, or do you feel the weariness of this vale of tears? What is your strongest thought, feeling, or desire?

Relate: Speak to the Shepherd about what is on your heart. Turn your attention from yourself to the Good Shepherd. Let him look at you with love.

Receive: What is in God's heart for you? Read the passage a third time. This time receive whatever the Good Shepherd wants to give or communicate to you.

Respond: Respond to whatever God gives you. Perhaps you need to let the Shepherd hold you. Maybe you just need to lie down for a little rest. Just be with the Lord for a minute or two before moving on.

SUGGESTIONS FOR JOURNALING

1. I found strength and comfort when …
2. True peace for me would look like …
3. I sensed God communicating to me …
4. God wants to give me …
5. I was able to receive God's gift of … (or I hesitate to accept God's gift because …)

After you've journaled, close with a brief conversation giving thanks to God for your prayer experience. Then pray an Our Father.

December 16 — Saturday

Saturday of the Second Week of Advent

REVIEW

I love looking back and savoring the blessings that I have received over the course of the week. If you prefer to meditate on Scripture today, you can repeat one of the meditations from the past week instead. Pick either the best one, where you found the most blessing, or the most challenging and dry meditation. You can repeat that meditation today and see what God wants to give you the second time.

Preparation: *Come, Holy Spirit, enlighten the eyes of my heart.* Be present to the God who is always present to you. Call to mind his loving care for you and spend the first minute of your prayer resting in the free, unearned gift of loving and being loved. Let gratitude rise in your heart.

Grace for the Day: Speaking of the heart, what is the desire of your heart? Try to notice what you most deeply desire. Then share it with God in your own words, being confident that he loves you and wants to give you every blessing.

Week in Review: Flip back through your past week's journal entries. As you do, notice what emerged in the conversation. Here are some questions to help you:

1. Where did I notice God, and what was he doing or saying?
2. How did I respond to what God was doing?
3. I really struggled with …
4. Prayer really seemed to click when …
5. I'm grateful for …
6. Now, at the end of this Second Week of Advent, what new meaning is Christmas taking on for me?

What image of God's loving presence sticks with you most strongly?

Conclude by conversing with God about your week. Acknowledge what you have been experiencing. Relate it to him. Receive what he wants to give you. Respond to him. Then savor that image of God's loving presence and rest there for a minute or two. Close with an Our Father.

Week Three

Countdown to Christmas

How was imaginative prayer? Some people love it, and some people struggle with it. While *lectio divina* can be used with any Scripture passage, imaginative prayer works best with passages that contain visuals and action. As we move forward, I'll use one or the other prayer form each day, depending on what I think fits with the passage. You don't have to follow my guidance. If you prefer one prayer form, you can use it all the time. But let me encourage you to try to become comfortable with both prayer forms. Remember that these two prayer forms are just conversation starters; it is the conversation itself that is key to a good prayer time. Good prayer is about spending quality time with God. If you have spent quality time with God at all this week, you have done well.

This year we have the shortest possible Advent. You may find it feels rushed or that you have a hard time settling in to a good prayer routine. You may also find yourself facing some discouragement or resistance. Just because there are difficulties does not mean that you are doing something wrong. In fact, just the opposite. A challenging journey is often a sign that you are on the right road. The harder the pilgrimage, the more fruitful it tends to be.

Perhaps your prayer times have not been as consistent as you had hoped, or maybe this Advent feels less prayerful than last year. Be patient with yourself, and don't let your expectations get in the way of your journey. I have walked many pilgrimages. There are lots of similarities from year to year, but each year is unique and special. Be open to the journey that God wants to give you and try not to judge or blame yourself or others if it isn't shaping up like you expected. Keep walking, and let's see what is coming around the next corner.

Nine days before Christmas, our pilgrimage switches gears. The lectionary gives us readings from the Gospel passages that immediately precede the birth of Jesus. Additionally, each day from December 17 to December 23 is assigned a special "O Antiphon," a poetic invocation that names who the coming Messiah is and what he will do, drawing on imagery from Old Testament prophecies. The Messiah is very close to us.

Grace of the Week: God has a plan to restore creation and undo the effects of sin. He plans to send us a Savior who is also his Son. In fact, as we wait and watch for the coming Messiah, we begin to realize that he is already here with us. Pray that your eyes may be opened to the presence of "Emmanuel," God-with-us, in your everyday life.

December 17 — Sunday

Third Sunday of Advent Countdown to Christmas: Nine

O Wisdom of our God Most High,
guiding creation with power and love:
come to teach us the path of knowledge!

Preparation: *Come, Holy Spirit, enlighten the eyes of my heart.* Remind your heart of God's loving presence and spend the first minute of your prayer resting in the free, unearned gift of loving and being loved. Let gratitude rise in your heart.

Set the Scene: Pray in your own words that your eyes may be opened to the presence of "Emmanuel," God-with-us, in your everyday life.

Read the passage. As you do, set the scene in your mind. John is clothed in camel's hair and eating locusts and wild honey. He is out in the wilderness preaching repentance. Crowds are gathering along the bank of the Jordan River to be baptized by him. Spend a few minutes building the scene in your imagination. What does the wilderness look like, feel like, smell like?

JOHN 1:6–8, 19–28 (LECTIONARY)

A man named John was sent from God. He came for testimony, to testify to the light, so that all might believe through him. He was not the light, but came to testify to the light.

And this is the testimony of John. When the Jews from Jerusalem sent priests and Levites to him to ask him, "Who are you?" he admitted and did not deny it, but admitted,

> *"I am not the Christ." So they asked him, "What are you then? Are you Elijah?" And he said, "I am not." "Are you the Prophet?" He answered, "No." So they said to him, "Who are you, so we can give an answer to those who sent us? What do you have to say for yourself?" He said: "I am* the voice of one crying out in the desert, 'Make straight the way of the Lord,' *as Isaiah the prophet said." Some Pharisees were also sent. They asked him, "Why then do you baptize if you are not the Christ or Elijah or the Prophet?" John answered them, "I baptize with water; but there is one among you whom you do not recognize, the one who is coming after me, whose sandal strap I am not worthy to untie." This happened in Bethany across the Jordan, where John was baptizing.*

Action! Read the passage a second time.

See the priests, Levites, and Pharisees approaching to question John. See John's confident response: The Messiah is already among us.

Place yourself in the scene. Feel the sun beating down on you and smell the Jordan River. Where are you most comfortable: Being with the crowds lining up for baptism? Are you among the priests and Pharisees? Are you sitting at a comfortable distance, watching it all unfold, but trying not to get involved?

Acknowledge: God's wisdom from on high has been guiding creation with power and love. But the wise of this world tend to miss God's plans because they think they already know the path of knowledge. Have you been humbly receiving God's plan for your Advent, or are you judging it like the priests and Levites are judging John? Notice what is going on inside of you — your thoughts, feelings, and desires.

Relate: The long-awaited Messiah is next to you, standing or sitting with you in the scene. How does that make you feel? Share with him what is on your heart. Let him look at you with love.

Shift your attention from yourself to him as you read the passage a third time.

Receive: Receive whatever is in God's heart for you — his thoughts, feelings, desires.

Respond: Have a conversation with Jesus as you sit on the bank of the river or wherever your imagination has taken you. Then just be with the Lord and enjoy his quiet presence for a minute or two before moving on.

SUGGESTIONS FOR JOURNALING

1. While imagining the scene, what stood out to me was …
2. When Jesus entered the scene I felt …
3. I sensed God communicating to me …
4. Jesus is with me when …
5. Jesus is calling me to …

After you've journaled, close with a brief conversation, giving thanks to God for your prayer experience. Then pray an Our Father.

December 18 — Monday

Countdown to Christmas: Eight

O Leader of the House of Israel,
giver of the Law of Moses on Sinai:
come to rescue us with your mighty power!

Preparation: Come, Holy Spirit, enlighten the eyes of my heart. Be present to the God who is always present to you. Call to mind his loving care for you and spend the first minute of your prayer resting in the free, unearned gift of loving and being loved. Let gratitude rise in your heart.

Set the Scene: Pray in your own words that your eyes may be opened to the presence of "Emmanuel," God-with-us, in your everyday life.

Read the passage. As you do, set the scene in your mind. Mary had gone to visit her cousin Elizabeth and was absent for three months (see Lk 1:56). On her return, she would have been visibly pregnant. Picture where Saint Joseph was when he learned this. What were his thoughts, feelings, and desires?

MATTHEW 1:18–25 (LECTIONARY)

This is how the birth of Jesus Christ came about. When his mother Mary was betrothed to Joseph, but before they lived together, she was found with child through the Holy Spirit. Joseph her husband, since he was a righteous man, yet unwilling to expose her to shame, decided to divorce her quietly. Such was his intention when, behold, the angel of the Lord appeared to him in a dream and said, "Joseph, son of David, do not be afraid to take Mary your wife into your home. For it is through the Holy Spirit that this child has been conceived in her. She will bear a son and you are to name him Jesus, because he will save his people from their sins." All this took place to fulfill what the Lord had said through the prophet:

> Behold, the virgin shall be with child and bear a son,
> and they shall name him Emmanuel,

which means "God is with us." When Joseph awoke, he did as the angel of the Lord had commanded him and took his wife into his home. He had no relations with her until she bore a son, and he named him Jesus.

Action! God gave the law that ultimately put Joseph in this difficult predicament. Yet God was also there to show him the way forward. What difference does it make that "God is with us"? How did God's loving presence in the situation change the meaning of that situation and the direction of Joseph's life? What did Joseph feel before and after his dream?

Acknowledge: Have you found yourself in a similarly impossible situation, where your "Yes" to God's will seemed to place you "between a rock and a hard place"? Or perhaps you have a friend, family member, or neighbor going through this kind of difficulty. How does it make you feel?

Read the passage a second time and notice your thoughts, feelings, and desires.

Relate: Speak to the Father about what is on your heart. Let him look at you with love. Know that God is "Emmanuel" in whatever situation you're experiencing. Just as sure as he was with Joseph, so surely God is with you right now.

Receive: How does it change the situation knowing God is with you?

Read the passage a third time. Receive whatever is in God's heart for you — his thoughts, feelings, desires.

Respond: Now answer him. Just be with the Lord for a minute or two before moving on.

SUGGESTIONS FOR JOURNALING

1. I found God in the midst of my struggles when …
2. My greatest fear or struggle seems to be …
3. I sensed God communicating to me …
4. God is with me in the way that …
5. Now that Christmas is just one week away, I feel God's love inviting me to a new way of seeing, thinking, or acting …

After you've journaled, close with a brief conversation with God, giving thanks for your prayer experience. Then pray an Our Father.

December 19 — Tuesday

Countdown to Christmas: Seven

O Root of Jesse's stem,
sign of God's love for all his people:
come to save us without delay!

Preparation: *Come, Holy Spirit, enlighten the eyes of my heart.* Be present to the God who is always present to you. Call to mind his loving care for you and spend the first minute of your prayer resting in the free, unearned gift of loving and being loved. Praise God in your heart for his unfailing goodness.

Set the Scene: Pray in your own words that your eyes may be opened to the presence of "Emmanuel," God-with-us, in your everyday life.

Read the passage. As you do, set the scene in your mind. What does the temple look like? What does the angel look like? Picture the people outside waiting for Zechariah to emerge.

LUKE 1:5–25 (LECTIONARY)

In the days of Herod, King of Judea, there was a priest named Zechariah of the priestly division of Abijah; his wife was from the daughters of Aaron, and her name was Elizabeth. Both were righteous in the eyes of God, observing all the commandments and ordinances of the Lord blamelessly. But they had no child, because Elizabeth was barren and both were advanced in years.

Once when he was serving as priest in his division's turn before God, according to the practice of the priestly service, he was chosen by lot to enter the sanctuary of the Lord to burn incense. Then, when the whole assembly of the people was praying outside at the hour of the incense offering, the angel of the Lord appeared to him, standing at the right of the altar of incense. Zechariah was troubled by what he saw, and fear came upon him.

But the angel said to him, "Do not be afraid, Zechariah, because your prayer has been heard. Your wife Elizabeth will bear you a son, and you shall name him John. And you will have joy and gladness, and many will rejoice at his birth, for he will be great in the sight of the Lord. He will drink neither wine nor strong drink. He will be filled with the Holy Spirit even from his mother's womb, and he will turn many of the children of Israel to the Lord their God. He will go before him in the spirit and power of Elijah to turn the hearts of fathers toward children and the disobedient to the understanding of the righteous, to prepare a people fit for the Lord."

Then Zechariah said to the angel, "How shall I know this? For I am an old man, and my wife is advanced in years." And the angel said to him in reply, "I am Gabriel, who stand before God. I was sent to speak to you and to announce to you this good news. But now you will be speechless and unable to talk until the day these things take place, because you did not believe my words, which will be fulfilled at their proper time."

Meanwhile the people were waiting for Zechariah and were amazed that he stayed so long in the sanctuary. But when he came out, he was unable to speak to them, and they realized that he had seen a vision in the sanctuary. He was gesturing to them but remained mute.

Then, when his days of ministry were completed, he went home.

After this time his wife Elizabeth conceived, and she went into seclusion for five months, saying, "So has the Lord done for me at a time when he has seen fit to take away my disgrace before others."

Action! Read the passage a second time and play the scene forward in your mind.

Today's antiphon is drawn from Isaiah 11:1–10. King David's line had long ago been "cut off" from royal power. But God will raise up a new shoot from the "stump of Jesse" (King David's father), and "his dwelling shall be glorious."

In a similar way, Zechariah and Elizabeth have long given up the dream of having a child of their own. Even though he is a priest ministering in the temple, Zechariah does not expect an angel. Even less is he prepared for the good news the angel brings.

Acknowledge: How does Zechariah feel about all this? How does Elizabeth feel? How do you feel? What is the desire of your heart?

Relate: Speak to the Father about the desires of your heart. Do you believe he will fulfill them? Let him look at you with love. Read the passage a third time.

Receive: Receive whatever is in God's heart for you — his thoughts, feelings, desires, his Good News for you. Do you believe that God can, and will, do good things in your life?

Respond: Continue the conversation. Then just be with the Lord for a minute or two before moving on.

SUGGESTIONS FOR JOURNALING

1. I felt God stirring up a desire for ...
2. I have a hard time trusting when ...
3. My greatest fear or struggle seems to be ...
4. I sensed God was with me and wanted me to know ...
5. I ended prayer with a deeper sense ...

After you've journaled, close with a brief conversation giving thanks to God for your prayer experience. Then pray an Our Father.

December 20 — Wednesday

Countdown to Christmas: Six

O Key of David,
opening the gates of God's eternal Kingdom:
come and free the prisoners of darkness!

Preparation: *Come, Holy Spirit, enlighten the eyes of my heart.* Be present to the God who is always present to you. Call to mind his loving care for you and spend the first minute of your prayer resting in the free, unearned gift of loving and being loved. Let gratitude rise in your heart.

Set the Scene: Pray that your eyes may be opened to the presence "Emmanuel," God-with-us, in your everyday life.

Read the passage through to set the scene in your mind. Tradition usually sets the Annunciation at Mary's home in Nazareth. What time of day was it? Perhaps Mary has paused from her chores for a little prayer time. Use your imagination.

LUKE 1:26–38 (LECTIONARY)

In the sixth month, the angel Gabriel was sent from God to a town of Galilee called Nazareth, to a virgin betrothed to a man named Joseph, of the house of David, and the virgin's name was Mary. And coming to her, he said, "Hail, full of grace! The Lord is with you." But she was greatly troubled at what was said and pondered what sort of greeting this might be. Then the angel said to her, "Do not be afraid, Mary, for you have found favor with God. Behold, you will conceive in your womb and bear a son, and you shall name him Jesus. He will be great and will be called Son of the Most High, and the Lord God will give him the throne of David his father, and he will rule over the house of Jacob forever, and of his Kingdom there will be no end."

But Mary said to the angel, "How can this be, since I have no relations with a man?" And the angel said to her in reply, "The Holy Spirit will come upon you, and the power of the Most High will overshadow you. Therefore the child to be born will be called holy, the Son of God. And behold, Elizabeth, your relative, has also conceived a son in her old age, and this is the sixth month for her who was called barren; for nothing will be impossible for God."

Mary said, "Behold, I am the handmaid of the Lord. May it be done to me according to your word." Then the angel departed from her.

Action! In those days, betrothal meant that Mary and Joseph had already celebrated their wedding ceremony, but the living together (and the marital relations that typically came with it) hadn't started yet.

Today's O Antiphon takes the Key of David (see Is 22:22) in two different directions: It will open the kingdom of heaven that was closed by Eve's sin, and it will unlock the prisoners who have been kept in darkness by that same sin. But the key doesn't have the power to unlock Mary's womb; only she can do that. All of creation, groaning under the sentence of sin, awaits her answer with bated breath.

Read the passage a second time and play the scene forward in your mind.

Acknowledge: Why is this virgin greatly troubled at the angel's words? What is in her heart at this moment? What does her "yes" feel like for her?

Relate: Do you sometimes have a hard time accepting God's plans for your life? Is God waiting for you to "unlock" your heart to him? Speak to Mary about your thoughts and feelings. Together with her, turn to the Father in prayer.

Read the passage a third time.

Receive: Receive whatever is in God's heart for you — his thoughts, feelings, desires. He did all this for you. What more does he want to give you?

Respond: Converse with the Father in your heart. Then just be with the Lord and with Mary for a minute or two before moving on.

SUGGESTIONS FOR JOURNALING

1. My heart is troubled by …
2. How have I responded when God seemed to interrupt my plans?
3. What I most noticed about Mary was …
4. I sensed God was with me and wanted me to know …
5. I ended prayer wanting …

After you've journaled, close with a brief conversation with God giving thanks for your prayer experience. Then pray a Hail Mary.

December 21 — Thursday

Countdown to Christmas: Five

O Radiant Dawn,
splendor of eternal light, sun of justice:
come and shine on those who dwell in
darkness and in the shadow of death.

Preparation: *Come, Holy Spirit, enlighten the eyes of my heart.* Be present to the God who is always present to you. Call to mind his loving care for you and spend the first minute of your prayer resting in the free, unearned gift of loving and being loved. Let gratitude rise in your heart.

Set the Scene: Pray in your own words that your eyes may be opened to the presence of "Emmanuel," God-with-us, in your everyday life.

Read the passage. Tradition identifies this location as a town called Ein Karem, a hill town about five miles to the west of Jerusalem and about ninety miles from Nazareth. Elizabeth is already six months pregnant. Mary hasn't started to show yet.

LUKE 1:39–45 (LECTIONARY)

Mary set out in those days and traveled to the hill country in haste to a town of Judah, where she entered the house of Zechariah and greeted Elizabeth. When Elizabeth heard Mary's greeting, the infant leaped in her womb, and Elizabeth, filled with the Holy Spirit, cried out in a loud voice and said, "Most blessed are you among women, and blessed is the fruit of your womb. And how does this happen to me, that the mother of my Lord should come to me? For at the moment the sound of your greeting reached my ears, the infant in my womb leaped for

> *joy. Blessed are you who believed that what was spoken to you by the Lord would be fulfilled."*

Action! "Emmanuel" means "God is with us" (Mt 1:23). How was God with Mary on her journey to visit Elizabeth? How does Elizabeth feel in the presence of her infant Lord?

Read the passage a second time and play the scene forward in your mind.

Acknowledge: Christmas is a busy time for visiting and receiving visitors. Do your visitors bring the presence of Jesus to your home, or do they bring worries of being judged for a messy home? When you visit others, how do you bring Jesus with you to their home? When did you leap for joy at God's presence in your life?

Relate: Let your thoughts and feelings rise to the surface. Speak to God what is in your heart. God the Father is also present in this scene and gazing with love upon these women whom he has blessed with the gift of life.

Picture the scene from God's perspective as you read the passage a third time.

Receive: How does the Father view this scene? How does he gaze upon your visits and visitors? Receive whatever is in God's heart for you — his thoughts, feelings, desires.

Respond: Converse with the Father in your heart. Then just savor the presence of Jesus for a minute or two before moving on.

SUGGESTIONS FOR JOURNALING

1. My heart leaped for joy when …
2. The holiday visitor that most brought Jesus to me was …
3. I sensed God saying to me …
4. I ended prayer wanting …
5. How can I "go in haste" to share with another the joy I am receiving through these Advent prayer times?

After you've journaled, close with a brief conversation with God giving thanks for your prayer experience. Then pray a Hail Mary.

December 22 — Friday

Countdown to Christmas: Four

O King of all nations and keystone of the Church:
come and save man, whom you formed from the dust!

Preparation: *Come, Holy Spirit, enlighten the eyes of my heart.* Be present to the God who is always present to you. Call to mind his loving care for you and spend the first minute of your prayer resting in the free, unearned gift of loving and being loved. Let gratitude rise in your heart.

***Lectio*:** Pray in your own words that your eyes may be opened to the presence of "Emmanuel," God-with-us, in your everyday life.

Read the passage slowly and prayerfully. This Scripture passage is called the Magnificat (the first word of the passage in Latin). It is a hymn of praise to God who has been faithful to his promises from Abraham until today. This could very well be a song that the saints sing in heaven. Is there one word or phrase that you feel moved to focus on?

LUKE 1:46–56 (LECTIONARY)

Mary said:
"My soul proclaims the greatness of the Lord;
my spirit rejoices in God my savior,
for he has looked upon his lowly servant.
From this day all generations will call me blessed:
the Almighty has done great things for me,
and holy is his Name.
He has mercy on those who fear him
in every generation.
He has shown the strength of his arm,
and has scattered the proud in their conceit.

He has cast down the mighty from their thrones
and has lifted up the lowly.
He has filled the hungry with good things,
and the rich he has sent away empty.
He has come to the help of his servant Israel
for he has remembered his promise of mercy,
the promise he made to our fathers,
to Abraham and his children for ever."
Mary remained with Elizabeth about three months and then returned to her home.

***Meditatio*:** Have you noticed recent news stories in which God humbled the proud or lifted up the lowly? How has God done great things for you? Have you experienced his mercy, blessing, or strength?

Or perhaps you feel lowly and humbled, like someone who needs to be raised from the dust. How are you waiting for the King of all nations to come rescue you with the might of his arm?

Reflect for a few minutes or just focus on the word or phrase that speaks to you. Then read the passage again slowly.

***Oratio*:** Speak to God what is on your heart and mind, your thoughts, feelings, and desires.

***Contemplatio*:** Open your heart to receive what God wants to give you. Maybe it is a thought, a word, or a sense of peace. God is with you in this ordinary moment. Even his challenging words come with love.

When you are done speaking, read the passage one more time. Rest in and savor God's loving presence with you. Be present. Be lowly.

SUGGESTIONS FOR JOURNALING

1. My favorite word or phrase was …
2. God fulfilled his promises to me when …
3. I rejoice in God my Savior when I recall …
4. I noticed God was with me this week when …
5. Mary takes Jesus with her wherever she goes. How can I take Jesus with me on my journey today?

After you've journaled, close with a brief conversation with God giving thanks for your prayer experience. Then read today's Scripture one more time as a prayer of praise.

December 23 — Saturday

Countdown to Christmas: Three

O Emmanuel, our King and Giver of Law:
come to save us, Lord our God!

Usually we would take Saturday to review our week. However, the Scripture passages are just too important to skip in this final countdown. We'll do a brief review after this meditation.

Preparation: *Come, Holy Spirit, enlighten the eyes of my heart.* Be present to the God who is always present to you. Call to mind his loving care for you and spend the first minute of your prayer resting in the free, unearned gift of loving and being loved. Let gratitude rise in your heart.

Set the Scene: Pray in your own words that your eyes may be opened to the presence of "Emmanuel," God-with-us, in your everyday life.

It's easy to imagine Elizabeth's neighbors and relatives gathering around to celebrate the birth of a healthy baby boy. The circumcision was like a baptism party. The name John means, "God is gracious." Set the scene in your imagination. Populate it with villagers.

LUKE 1:57–66 (LECTIONARY)

When the time arrived for Elizabeth to have her child she gave birth to a son. Her neighbors and relatives heard that the Lord had shown his great mercy toward her, and they rejoiced with her. When they came on the eighth day to circumcise the child, they were going to call him Zechariah after his father, but his mother said in reply, "No. He will be called John." But they answered her, "There is no one among your relatives who has this name." So they made signs, asking his father what he wished him to be called. He asked for a tablet and wrote, "John is his name," and all were amazed. Immediately his mouth was opened, his tongue freed, and he spoke blessing God. Then fear came upon all their neighbors, and all these matters were discussed throughout the hill country of Judea. All who heard these things took them to heart, saying, "What, then, will this child be?" For surely the hand of the Lord was with him.

Action! Zechariah is a silent participant — imagine the look on his face as he meets his son and welcomes his guests. Imagine the look on everyone's face when suddenly he can speak again!

Even though Mary isn't mentioned, she was probably in the crowd somewhere — why else would she have remained for three months with Elizabeth? Where are you in the crowd?

Acknowledge: Read the passage a second time.

How do you feel at the birth of John the Baptist, who will prepare the way for the King of all nations and keystone of the Church? What thoughts and feelings rise to the surface?

Relate: Speak to God what is in your heart. If you have a hard time expressing yourself, maybe Zechariah can help.

Receive: Read the passage a third time.

Receive whatever is in God's heart for you — his thoughts, feelings, desires. Does your heavenly Father look at you like Zechariah looked at his son, John?

Respond: Let the Father look at you and look back at him. Just savor the joy of being your Father's child for a minute or two before moving on.

SUGGESTIONS FOR JOURNALING

1. The part that most struck me about this passage was …
2. When do I feel tongue-tied? Or was there something today that I had a hard time receiving and accepting?

3. The look of the Father said to me …
4. I ended prayer wanting …
5. I have a new appreciation for …

A BRIEF REVIEW

Take a little time at the end of your prayer today and flip back through the previous week.

1. How has God been present to me in the midst of the season's busyness?
2. Is there a particular theme that is emerging on my Advent pilgrimage?
3. What helps me stay present to God throughout the day, after my prayer time is done?
4. During the final rush to Christmas, I desire most deeply …
5. The clearest and most powerful image of God's love for me has been …

Acknowledge what you have been experiencing. Relate it to him. Receive what he wants to give you. Respond to him. Then savor that image of God's loving presence and rest there for a minute or two. Close with an Our Father.

Week Four

Lord, When Did You Get Here?

(see John 6:25)

"Be watchful! Be alert! You do not know when the time will come" (Mk 13:33). Our Advent season began with these words. Holy Mother Church tells us to get ready to celebrate the coming of Christ on December 25, and we also prepare our hearts for the Second Coming of Christ. We gaze off into the distance, eagerly scanning the horizon to catch a glimpse of the Master. Then we notice, to our surprise, that he is already here.

I fully expect that you have had this experience on your Advent journey. Whether in prayer time or in the moments of everyday life, Jesus continues to be Emmanuel, God with us. We think that God needs to come to us. But the truth is that our eyes must be opened to his constant, quiet, humble presence.

After one walking pilgrimage, three of us were interviewed by Relevant Radio. The host said, "It must be an amazing experience when you finally walk into the shrine after all those miles."

The pilgrims looked at each other.

"It's not like you are waiting the whole time for one big payout at the end," I said.

"You get a lot of graces and blessings along the way," said another.

"Yes, there's a great feeling of joy and relief when you finish, but the pilgrimage is about more than that," said the third pilgrim.

With a walking pilgrimage, it isn't just the destination that matters. You are changed by the journey. This is precisely why *Oriens* is *a pilgrimage* through Advent and Christmas. I firmly believe that the daily prayer time you have invested in is opening the eyes of your heart to the presence of Jesus alive and active in your life. Jesus has always been with us, we just didn't know how to see him.

We have one final preparation day in this shortest-possible Advent season. Then the Christmas celebration begins. I say it "begins" because the feast of Christmas is too big to fit into one day. For eight days we celebrate the long-awaited Radiant Dawn, the Sun of Justice, and King of all nations who is Christ the Lord. I tell school children that the Octave of Christmas means you have to eat Christmas treats every day for eight days.

The Gloria is sung at Mass for all eight days of the octave. Several of these days are special feast days dedicated to particular saints. Celebrate Christmas by swapping out the purple and pink candles on your Advent wreath for white candles. Light them when you eat your family meals and sing a Christmas carol together each time. And keep making time for your pilgrimage! We've come through Advent and have only begun to journey through Christmas.

Grace of the Week: Our readings will be drawn from the Lectionary's readings for each feast or for the daily Mass readings. Ask God for a deeper experience of the Love that is Emmanuel, God-with-us, that your heart may be filled with warmth and light.

December 24 — Sunday

Fourth Sunday of Advent, Countdown to Christmas: Two

O Radiant Dawn, splendor of eternal light,
Sun of Justice: come and shine on those who dwell
in darkness and in the shadow of death.

Preparation: *Come, Holy Spirit, enlighten the eyes of my heart.* Be present to the God who is always present to you. Call to mind his loving care for you and spend the first minute of your prayer resting in the free, unearned gift of loving and being loved. Let gratitude rise in your heart.

***Lectio*:** We will use the Scripture reading from December 24 instead of the Gospel for the Fourth Sunday of Advent. Zechariah hasn't spoken for nine months — and now he has a lot to say! He knows that Jesus has come to set us free from a slavery far greater than that of the Israelites in Egypt or oppression by the Romans.

Read this passage slowly and prayerfully. Is there a word or phrase that speaks to you most strongly?

LUKE 1:67–79 (LECTIONARY)

Zechariah his father, filled with the Holy Spirit,
prophesied, saying:
"Blessed be the Lord, the God of Israel;
for he has come to his people and set them free.
He has raised up for us a mighty Savior,
born of the house of his servant David.
Through his prophets he promised of old
that he would save us from our enemies,

from the hands of all who hate us.
He promised to show mercy to our fathers
and to remember his holy covenant.
This was the oath he swore to our father Abraham:
to set us free from the hand of our enemies,
free to worship him without fear,
holy and righteous in his sight all the days of our life.
You, my child, shall be called the prophet of the Most High,
for you will go before the Lord to prepare his way,
to give his people knowledge of salvation
by the forgiveness of their sins.
In the tender compassion of our God
the dawn from on high shall break upon us,
to shine on those who dwell in darkness and the shadow of death,
and to guide our feet into the way of peace."

***Meditatio*:** *O Radiant Dawn*! The dawn from on high that shall break upon us. You guessed it, that is the word *Oriens*. With this being the day before Christmas, it is as though the dawn is just starting to peek out over the hills. Have you felt God's light shining more brightly as you draw close to Christmas? Has God been guiding your feet into the way of peace?

Read the passage a second time, or maybe just the part that speaks to you.

***Oratio*:** What do you want to say to God, with the birth of his Son so close at hand? Speak to God what is on your heart and mind. When you are done speaking, read the passage a third time and soak it in.

***Contemplatio*:** Read the passage one more time. Open your heart to receive what God wants to give you. God loves every child like an only child. Rest in and savor his love for you. Let the dawn from on high shine upon you. Bask in the light of God's love for a few minutes before moving on.

SUGGESTIONS FOR JOURNALING

1. God has set me free from …
2. I experienced the forgiveness of sins in a personal way when …
3. I feel the light of God shining in my heart when …
4. God's love feels like …
5. I need patience as I wait for …

After you've journaled, close with a brief conversation with God giving thanks for your prayer experience. Then close by reading today's Scripture one more time as a prayer of praise.

Announcement of the Birth of Christ

The text below, taken from the Roman Martyrology, presents the birth of Jesus as one would announce the birth of a king or emperor. The announcement is recited or chanted on December 24 during the celebration of the Liturgy of the Hours or before Christmas Mass during the night.

The Twenty-fifth Day of December, when ages beyond number had run their course from the creation of the world, when God in the beginning created heaven and earth, and formed man in his own likeness;

when century upon century had passed since the Almighty set his bow in the clouds after the Great Flood, as a sign of covenant and peace;

in the twenty-first century since Abraham, our father in faith, came out of Ur of the Chaldees;

in the thirteenth century since the People of Israel were led by Moses in the Exodus from Egypt;

around the thousandth year since David was anointed King;

in the sixty-fifth week of the prophecy of Daniel;

in the one hundred and ninety-fourth Olympiad;

in the year seven hundred and fifty-two since the foundation of the City of Rome;

in the forty-second year of the reign of Caesar Octavian Augustus, the whole world being at peace,

Jesus Christ, eternal God and Son of the eternal Father, desiring to consecrate the world by his most loving presence, was conceived by the Holy Spirit, and when nine months had passed since his conception, was born of the Virgin Mary in Bethlehem of Judah, and was made man:

The Nativity of Our Lord Jesus Christ according to the flesh.

(Appendix 1 of the Roman Missal, Third Edition)

December 25 — Monday

The Nativity of Our Lord Jesus Christ

Preparation: *Come, Holy Spirit, enlighten the eyes of my heart.* Be present to the God who is always present to you. Call to mind his loving care for you and spend the first minute of your prayer resting in the free, unearned gift of loving and being loved. Let gratitude rise in your heart.

Set the Scene: Ask God for a deeper experience of the Love that is Emmanuel, God-with-us, that your heart may be filled with warmth and light.

We like to think of the Nativity as something easy, peaceful, and cozy. But our Gospel implies crowds thronging to fulfill the decree, a long journey on dusty roads with a very pregnant woman, and finding yourself homeless at the most inopportune time. Read through the Gospel to set the scene in your imagination.

LUKE 2:1–20

In those days a decree went out from Caesar Augustus that the whole world should be enrolled. This was the first enrollment, when Quirinius was governor of Syria. So all went to be enrolled, each to his own town. And Joseph too went up from Galilee from the town of Nazareth to Judea, to the city of David that is called Bethlehem, because he was of the house and family of David, to be enrolled with Mary, his betrothed, who was with child. While they were there, the time came for her to have her child, and she gave birth to her firstborn son. She wrapped him in swaddling clothes and laid him in a manger, because there was no room for them in the inn. Now there were shepherds in that region living in the fields and keeping the night watch over their flock. The angel of the Lord appeared to them and the glory of the Lord shone around them, and they were struck with great fear. The angel said to them, "Do not be afraid; for behold, I proclaim to you good news of great joy that will be for all the people. For today in the city of David a savior has been born for you who is Messiah and Lord. And this will be a sign for you: you will find an infant wrapped in swaddling clothes and lying in a manger." And suddenly there was a multitude of the heavenly host with the angel, praising God and saying:

> *"Glory to God in the highest*
> *and on earth peace to those on whom his favor rests."*

When the angels went away from them to heaven, the shepherds said to one another, "Let us go, then, to Bethlehem to see this thing that has taken place, which the Lord has made known to us." So they went in haste and found Mary and Joseph, and the infant lying in the manger.

When they saw this, they made known the message that had been told them about this child. All who heard it were amazed by what had been told them by the shepherds.

And Mary kept all these things, reflecting on them in her heart. Then the shepherds returned, glorifying and praising God for all they had heard and seen, just as it had been told to them.

Action! Play the scene forward in your mind. World events collide to bring the little family to their hometown to fulfill an ancient prophecy regarding the birthplace of the Messiah. God provides an unorthodox, but effective, bed for his little Son. God "lifts up the lowly" by inviting humble shepherds to come and adore the newborn king. Where do you find yourself in this scene?

Acknowledge: Read the passage a second time. You are watching God fulfill his promise of mercy. What is in Mary's heart? Joseph's heart? The hearts of the shepherds? Your heart?

Relate: Speak to God what is in your heart. You could also speak to Mary about what this moment is like to her, or talk to the infant Christ.

Receive: Read the passage a third time. Receive whatever is in God's heart for you. Perhaps you can ask Mary to let you hold her child. What rises up in your heart as you receive the Savior?

Respond: Savor the joy of holding the Son and being held by the Father for a little while.

SUGGESTIONS FOR JOURNALING

1. I saw God's love particularly when …
2. The glory of the Lord shone at Christmas when …
3. The Father seemed to be saying to me …
4. I was surprised by …
5. My heart rested when …

After you've journaled, close with a brief conversation with God about your prayer experience. Then pray an Our Father.

December 26 — Tuesday

Second Day in the Octave of Christmas

SAINT STEPHEN, DEACON AND MARTYR

Stephen was one of seven men chosen to be the first deacons of the infant Church (see Acts 6:1–6). He did great wonders and signs, and preached the Gospel with so much wisdom that his opponents were confounded. They falsely accused him of blasphemy, and a mob stoned him to death (see Acts 6:8—8:1).

Stephen is the first in a long line of faithful servants who gave their lives in witness to the true King. This feast reminds us that Jesus was born into time so that Stephen, and all of us, could be born into eternity.

Preparation: *Come, Holy Spirit, enlighten the eyes of my heart.* Be present to the God who is always present to you. Call to mind his loving care for you and spend the first minute of your prayer resting in the free, unearned gift of loving and being loved. Let gratitude rise in your heart.

***Lectio*:** Ask God for a deeper experience of the Love that is Emmanuel, God-with-us, that your heart may be filled with warmth and light. Our Scripture today is the psalm that is given for the feast day of Saint Stephen. The refrain that is given for this psalm is, "Into your hands, O Lord, I commend my spirit." You will immediately notice that when Jesus said his last words on the cross, he was quoting this Scripture. What else might it have in store for us? Read the passage slowly and prayerfully.

PSALM 31:3CD–4, 6 AND 8AB, 16BC AND 17 (LECTIONARY)

Be my rock of refuge,
a stronghold to give me safety.
You are my rock and my fortress;
for your name's sake you will lead and guide me.

Into your hands I commend my spirit;
you will redeem me, O Lord, O faithful God.
I will rejoice and be glad because of your mercy.
Rescue me from the clutches of my enemies
and my persecutors.
Let your face shine upon your servant;
save me in your kindness.

***Meditatio*:** One day we celebrate the peace and joy of Christmas, and the next day we are celebrating a martyrdom. Why would the Church celebrate the first martyr on the day after Christmas?

Jesus is entering occupied territory. The world belongs to his Father, but the Enemy has usurped the throne and claimed it for himself. Jesus is returning to reclaim what is rightfully his. His birth is like an invasion of grace and light into a dark world full of sin. We should not be surprised that the Enemy would fight back. The faithful servants of the infant king will have to be prepared to serve him even unto death.

Was there anything in this passage that stood out to you? Read it again, slowly and prayerfully.

***Oratio*:** The face of God does in fact shine upon Stephen. He sees "the glory of God and Jesus standing at the right hand of God" (Acts 7:55). Do you believe enough in God to commend your spirit to him, as Stephen does? Notice your thoughts, feelings, and desires. Turn to God and share with him whatever is on your heart.

***Contemplatio*:** Read the passage a third time. This time, receive whatever is in God's heart for you. What does he desire for you? Spend a minute or two just being present to the faithful God who redeemed Stephen and will also redeem you.

SUGGESTIONS FOR JOURNALING

1. I was surprised by …
2. God wanted me to know that …
3. I saw the glory of God when …
4. How have I experienced an "invasion of grace and light" this

Christmas season?

5. God is faithful. In what way does Stephen's witness inspire me to be faithful?

After you've journaled, close with a brief conversation with God about your prayer experience. Then pray an Our Father.

December 27 — Wednesday

Third Day in the Octave of Christmas

SAINT JOHN, APOSTLE AND EVANGELIST

Born in Bethsaida on the Sea of Galilee, the brother of James and a fisherman by trade, John was called to follow Jesus while mending his nets (see Mk 1:19–20). Along with his brother James and fellow fisherman Peter, he was present at the Transfiguration of the Lord (Mk 9:2–8). The Gospel that bears his name refers to him only as "the Beloved Disciple." He was the one who reclined next to Jesus at the Last Supper (Jn 13:23) and stood at the foot of the cross as Jesus died. Jesus entrusted his mother to John's care (Jn 19:26–27). He wrote the fourth Gospel, penned three epistles, and is credited with the Book of Revelation. He was the only apostle not to be martyred. Tradition holds that he was miraculously preserved from attempts to kill him and died in exile on the Island of Patmos.

Preparation: *Come, Holy Spirit, enlighten the eyes of my heart.* Be present to the God who is always present to you. Call to mind his loving care for you and spend the first minute of your prayer resting in the free, unearned gift of loving and being loved. Let gratitude rise in your heart.

Set the Scene: Ask God for a deeper experience of the Love that is Emmanuel, God-with-us, that your heart may be filled with warmth and light.

There are places where we expect to find God's loving presence shining brightly (Christmas, a church, a birthday) and places where we expect not to find God's love shining (sin, death). But the Christmas story is a story of light shining in darkness. From a stable-cave to a tomb-cave, from swaddling clothes to burial cloths, from shepherds to fishermen, the story of the Christ is a story of happy surprises. Be prepared to be surprised by God's loving care today.

Jesus died on Good Friday and was buried in a new tomb. The disciples went into hiding to escape a similar fate. Now it's early Sunday morning (the first day of the week), and the tomb is suddenly empty. Picture the rock-hewn cave with a large stone rolled away, and dawn's light shining on the empty burial cloths. Read the passage slowly and prayerfully.

JOHN 20:1–8 (LECTIONARY)

On the first day of the week, Mary Magdalene ran and went to Simon Peter and to the other disciple whom Jesus loved, and told them, "They have taken the Lord from the tomb, and we do not know where they put him." So Peter and the other disciple went out and came to the tomb. They both ran, but the other disciple ran faster than Peter and arrived at the tomb first; he bent down and saw the burial cloths there, but did not go in. When Simon Peter arrived after him, he went into the tomb and saw the burial cloths there, and the cloth that had covered his head, not with the burial cloths but rolled up in a separate place. Then the other disciple also went in, the one who had arrived at the tomb first, and he saw and believed.

Action! Multiple times in the months leading up to the crucifixion, Jesus had predicted his passion, death, and resurrection (see Mk 8:31–33; 9:30–32; 10:32–34). The disciples, however, are so focused on the idea that Jesus will be a glorious king (Mk 10:35–45), that they cannot digest his message. What is Mary Magdalene thinking and feeling? How about Peter? John?

Read the Gospel a second time and notice what is going on with each character.

Acknowledge: How would you feel if three days after Grandma's funeral, you returned to the cemetery to find her grave dug up, her casket opened, and nothing inside but the clothes she had been buried in? What does the Resurrection feel like as a present reality? Be present to the story today.

Relate: The Risen Jesus has not abandoned his disciples. In just a few more lines, he will surprise Mary Magdalene with his loving presence (Jn 20:11–18). The Risen Jesus is with you right now. Turn to him. Share with him what is in your heart.

Receive: Read the passage a third time. What does Jesus want to share with you? Be with him and receive what is in his heart for you. Our God is a God of surprises. Allow yourself to be surprised by the peace, joy, and Good News that God wants to give you today.

Respond: Continue the conversation with him. Then be present with him for a minute or two and savor the Light who is life and love.

SUGGESTIONS FOR JOURNALING

1. I was surprised by …
2. I have a hard time finding God in my darkness because …
3. I have seen God's light shining in my darkness when …
4. The presence of the Risen Jesus gives me …
5. Jesus wanted me to know, experience, or realize that …
6. As a result of today's prayer time, I find myself more able to believe that …

After you've journaled, let the message of today's prayer experience sink into your heart and fill you with light and gratitude. Then pray an Our Father.

December 28 — Thursday

Fourth Day in the Octave of Christmas

THE HOLY INNOCENTS, MARTYRS

"The *flight into Egypt* and the massacre of the innocents make manifest the opposition of darkness to the light: 'He came to his own home, and his own people received him not.' Christ's whole life was lived under the sign of persecution. His own share it with him. Jesus' departure from Egypt recalls the exodus and presents him as the definitive liberator of God's people." (*Catechism of the Catholic Church* 530)

Preparation: *Come, Holy Spirit, enlighten the eyes of my heart.* Be present to the God who is always present to you. Call to mind his loving care for you and spend the first minute of your prayer resting in the free, unearned gift of loving and being loved. Let gratitude rise in your heart.

Set the Scene: Ask God for a deeper experience of the Love that is Emmanuel, God-with-us, that your heart may be filled with warmth and light.

The warmth and light of God's love enters a world full of corruption and selfishness. The current "king of the Jews" sees the true king as a threat to his power. Matthew wants us to think of Pharaoh, the great enemy of God's plans, who had all the Hebrew boys thrown into the Nile River (see Ex 1:22). Rather than a senseless killing, tradition has painted this feast as God confounding the mighty King Herod with a small army of tiny martyrs. An ancient sermon says, "They cannot use their limbs to engage in battle, yet already they bear off the palm of victory."

MATTHEW 2:13–18 (LECTIONARY)

When the magi had departed, behold, the angel of the Lord appeared to Joseph in a dream and said, "Rise, take the child and his mother, flee to Egypt, and stay there until I tell you. Herod is going to search for the child to de-

stroy him." Joseph rose and took the child and his mother by night and departed for Egypt. He stayed there until the death of Herod, that what the Lord had said through the prophet might be fulfilled, Out of Egypt I called my son.

When Herod realized that he had been deceived by the magi, he became furious. He ordered the massacre of all the boys in Bethlehem and its vicinity two years old and under, in accordance with the time he had ascertained from the magi. Then was fulfilled what had been said through Jeremiah the prophet:

> A voice was heard in Ramah,
> sobbing and loud lamentation;
> *Rachel weeping for her children,*
> *and she would not be consoled,*
> *since they were no more.*

Action! Play the scene forward in your mind. The Bible does not flinch to recount human depravity. It makes clear, however, that while God allows evil things to happen, he never causes them. He always works to bring good out of evil. How is God's loving care present in this difficult scene?

Acknowledge: What was this experience like for Mary and Joseph? What was it like for Jesus to grow up in exile outside his homeland, then to be the new kid in Nazareth? What thoughts, feelings, and desires are rising in your heart? Do you have any experience in your life that felt similar to the emotions expressed here?

Read the passage a second time.

Relate: Speak to God what is in your heart, even if you feel angry at him. Share the burden with him. Look at him and let him look at you.

Receive: Read the passage a third time. What does God want to say to you, or how does he lift your burden? Be open to receiving his answers.

Respond: How does God's response change your perspective? Receive what he has to give you, then rest in the Father's love for you, the same love that the Father has for his Son.

SUGGESTIONS FOR JOURNALING

1. How is God's light shining in the midst of darkness?
2. What new way of thinking or responding am I being invited to accept?
3. How have I personally experienced darkness, confusion, what seemed like a senseless "death"?
4. How has God's light shone in my darkness?
5. How is God calling me out of darkness, as he did Joseph?

After you've journaled, close with a brief conversation with God giving thanks for the warmth and light of your prayer experience. Then pray an Our Father.

December 29 — Friday

Fifth Day in the Octave of Christmas

ST. THOMAS BECKET

Thomas Becket was born in London in 1118. Though a cleric of the diocese of Canterbury, he became chancellor to King Henry II and took a leading part in a military expedition against the French. When the archbishop died, Thomas was chosen as his replacement. Perhaps Henry wanted "his man" to be chief cleric in England.

However, Thomas took his new responsibilities very seriously and began a life of penance and simplicity. He led a protracted defense of the Church's independence from the crown, which resulted in six years of exile. On this day in 1170, knights and a band of armed men slew him in his church. King Henry did public penance for this crime.

Preparation: *Come, Holy Spirit, enlighten the eyes of my heart.* Be present to the God who is always present to you. Call to mind his loving care for you and spend the first minute of your prayer resting in the free, unearned gift of loving and being loved. Let gratitude rise in your heart.

***Lectio*:** Ask God for a deeper experience of the Love that is Emmanuel, God-with-us, that your heart may be filled with warmth and light.

Read the passage through once. New life flows from a relationship with God. But that life must overflow into new relationships with others, my brothers and sisters. The new commandment is "As I [Jesus] have loved you, so you also should love one another" (Jn 13:34). Notice what word or phrase strikes you.

1 JOHN 2:3–11 (LECTIONARY)

Beloved: The way we may be sure that we know Jesus is to keep his commandments. Whoever says, "I know him," but does not keep his commandments is a liar, and the truth is not in him. But whoever keeps his word, the love of God is truly perfected in him. This is the way we may know that we are in union with him: whoever claims to abide in him ought to walk just as he walked.

Beloved, I am writing no new commandment to you but an old commandment that you had from the beginning. The old commandment is the word that you have heard. And yet I do write a new commandment to you, which holds true in him and among you, for the darkness is passing away, and the true light is already shining. Whoever says he is in the light, yet hates his brother, is still in the darkness. Whoever loves his brother remains in the light, and there is nothing in him to cause a fall. Whoever hates his brother is in darkness; he walks in darkness and does not know where he is going because the darkness has blinded his eyes.

***Meditatio*:** Read the passage again. Union with God is the whole point of the Gospel. And union with God will lead to love for one another. When do you find loving hard?

***Oratio*:** Talk to God about this call to keep his commandments and love your brother or sister. How do you struggle? When have you experienced victory? What help do you need from God? Ask for it.

***Contemplatio*:** Read the passage a third time. Receive what is in God's heart for you: his thoughts and feelings and desires. Spend some time experiencing more deeply God's loving presence with you and within you.

SUGGESTIONS FOR JOURNALING

1. The person I find hardest to love is …
2. I find God's love growing when …
3. These few weeks have helped me …
4. Communion with God feels like …
5. I ended prayer wanting …

After you've journaled, close by giving thanks to God for the warmth and light of your prayer time today and then end with an Our Father.

December 30 — Saturday

Sixth Day in the Octave of Christmas

REVIEW

In addition to the review below, or in place of it, you could choose to repeat any one of the meditations from the past week, if you find that to be a fruitful exercise.

Preparation: *Come, Holy Spirit, enlighten the eyes of my heart.* Call to mind God's loving care for you and spend the first minute of your prayer resting in the free, unearned gift of loving and being loved. Let gratitude rise in your heart.

Grace for the Day: What is the desire of your heart? Try to notice what you most deeply desire. Then share it with God in your own words, being confident that he loves you and wants to give you every blessing.

Week in Review: Flip back through your past week's journal entries. As you do, notice what emerged in the conversation. Here are some questions to help you:

1. Where did I notice God, and what was he doing or saying?
2. How did I respond to what God was doing?
3. I felt God's love most strongly when …
4. I found myself struggling with …
5. I'm grateful for …

Now go back to your journal entries from the First Sunday of Advent and then the last few Saturday reviews.

1. What did I desire as I began this journey? Have those desires grown or changed in some way?
2. Do I notice a particular theme that has been emerging on my Advent pilgrimage?
3. Do I have recurring fears or struggles that Jesus wants to address with me?
4. This Christmas, God has given me the gift of …
5. How has this Advent journey changed me?
6. My strongest sense, image, moment, or experience of God's loving presence was …

Acknowledge what you have been experiencing. Relate it to him. Receive what he wants to give you. Respond to him. Then savor that image of God's loving presence and rest there for a minute or two. Close with an Our Father.

Week Five

Well Begun Is Half Done

On my thirty-day silent retreat, I was introduced to the words of Saint Ignatius. He told retreatants to begin each prayer time by "Pausing for the space of an *Our Father* and considering how God Our Lord looks upon us." I wasn't sure how to do that. I tried various images of God's love, but it never really clicked for me, nor for the people I directed on retreats. I have realized this movement is essential. If we don't start prayer by realizing we are not alone, we might never actually get to conversation with God. Prayer will become nothing more than a conversation with myself, with me reading spiritual things and thinking up spiritual goals for myself. So what did Ignatius mean, and how do we do it?

In the course of writing this book, I stumbled on an answer to this question. A life of faith will eventually lead to experiences of God's love for you. They may be found in a particularly moving prayer time, an experience outside of prayer, an image, a Scripture passage, or even song lyrics. You can save this moment and reuse it the next time you go to prayer. Saint Ignatius's invitation isn't about inventing how God might look at me, but rather returning to a place where I have encountered God's love for me.

After I had this realization, the "colloquy" of Saint Ignatius at the end of prayer began to make more sense. Before we finish our prayer time, we should end with gratitude. When we realize what God has done for us, how he has loved us faithfully and sent his Son to die for us, we cannot help but feel grateful. Gratitude is the antidote to anger, the antithesis of a consumer mentality, and the right attitude of a disciple. Our prayer should begin and end with gratitude.

Mother Church has the same idea when we traditionally pray both a grace before meals and a grace after meals. Our meals, however meager they may be, begin and end with gratitude. The Church's Morning Prayer is called "Morning Praises" (*laudes*) to begin our day with gratitude. Night prayer ends with a hymn to Our Lady, an act of gratitude for her maternal care. The word *Eucharist* means "thanksgiving," as we begin and end our week with gratitude. For the last several years, I have kept a quart jar in my prayer space. Every Saturday, I write down the thing I am most grateful for and put it in the jar. At the end of the year, I dump out the jar and sift through all my blessings. Our meals, prayer time, days, weeks, and years should begin with gratitude and end with gratitude.

Grace of the Week: We will journey through the last official week of Christmas to the feasts of Epiphany and the Baptism of the Lord. Our guide will be the beloved disciple, who wrote both the Gospel of John and also three letters. He has a deep sense of God's love for us and a desire that you remain in that love and not reject it. Ask God for the grace both to experience and to live more deeply your true identity as a beloved child of God.

December 31 — Sunday

Seventh Day in the Octave of Christmas

The Holy Family of Jesus, Mary, and Joseph

Preparation: *Come, Holy Spirit, enlighten the eyes of my heart.* Be present to the God who is always present to you. Call to mind his loving care for you and spend the first minute of your prayer resting in the free, unearned gift of loving and being loved. Let gratitude rise in your heart.

Set the Scene: Ask God for the grace both to experience and to live more deeply your true identity as a beloved child of God.

Jewish law considered a mother unclean for forty days after giving birth to a male child (see Lv 12:1–8). She would then offer the sacrifice of a lamb. The Holy Family was too poor to afford a lamb, so they were permitted to offer two small birds instead.

The location is the majestic and most sacred temple in Jerusalem. For centuries the unseen God has been worshiped here. Now in the person of Jesus, God himself has come to visit his temple. Only an old man and an old woman recognize this momentous occasion. They symbolize the longing for God in every human heart, and faithful Israel grown old awaiting its Savior. They also remind us of all the elderly who faithfully worship God and trust in his promises.

Read the passage slowly and prayerfully to set the scene in your mind.

LUKE 2:22–40 (LECTIONARY)

When the days were completed for their purification according to the law of Moses, they took him up to Jerusalem to present him to the Lord, just as it is written in the law of the Lord, Every male that opens the womb shall be consecrated to the Lord, *and to offer the sacrifice of a*

pair of turtledoves or two young pigeons, in accordance with the dictate in the law of the Lord.
Now there was a man in Jerusalem whose name was Simeon. This man was righteous and devout, awaiting the consolation of Israel, and the Holy Spirit was upon him. It had been revealed to him by the Holy Spirit that he should not see death before he had seen the Christ of the Lord. He came in the Spirit into the temple; and when the parents brought in the child Jesus to perform the custom of the law in regard to him, he took him into his arms and blessed God, saying:

> *"Now, Master, you may let your servant go*
> *in peace, according to your word,*
> *for my eyes have seen your salvation,*
> *which you prepared in sight of all the peoples,*
> *a light for revelation to the Gentiles,*
> *and glory for your people Israel."*

The child's father and mother were amazed at what was said about him; and Simeon blessed them and said to Mary his mother, "Behold, this child is destined for the fall and rise of many in Israel, and to be a sign that will be contradicted — and you yourself a sword will pierce — so that the thoughts of many hearts may be revealed." There was also a prophetess, Anna, the daughter of Phanuel, of the tribe of Asher. She was advanced in years, having lived seven years with her husband after her marriage, and then as a widow until she was eighty-four. She never left the temple, but worshiped night and day with fasting and prayer. And coming forward at that very time, she gave thanks to God and spoke about the child to all who were awaiting the redemption of Jerusalem.

When they had fulfilled all the prescriptions of the law of the Lord, they returned to Galilee, to their own town of Nazareth. The child grew and became strong, filled with wisdom; and the favor of God was upon him.

Action! See the glorious, majestic temple. See the family too poor to offer a lamb, yet bearing in their hands the Lamb of God who will one day offer the perfect sacrifice foreshadowed by the temple worship. How do you feel as you witness the priests and people going about their business, oblivious to the Word-made-Flesh among them?

Now, focus on Mary, Joseph, Simeon, and Anna. What is in the heart of each person in the scene — what are they thinking and how are they feeling?

Read the passage a second time and notice the part that most speaks to you.

Acknowledge: What thoughts, feelings, and desires are in your heart?

Relate: Speak to God what is in your heart.

Receive: Listen to what the Holy Spirit wants to reveal to you in today's prayer. Read the passage a third time, or just the part that most speaks to you. Will Mary let you hold the Christ Child?

Respond: Give thanks to God and bless him in your own words. Then spend a minute or two savoring the loving presence of God present with you today.

SUGGESTIONS FOR JOURNALING

1. I was surprised by …
2. The part that most spoke to me was …
3. What am I waiting for God to give me? Am I patient, or anxious?
4. Do I desire to be filled with the Holy Spirit like Simeon?
5. I ended prayer wanting …

After you've journaled, close with a brief conversation with God giving thanks for your prayer experience. Then read Simeon's words again as a prayer:

> "Now, Master, you may let your servant go
> in peace, according to your word,
> for my eyes have seen your salvation,
> which you prepared in sight of all the peoples,
> a light for revelation to the Gentiles,
> and glory for your people Israel."

January 1 — Monday

The Blessed Virgin Mary, the Mother of God

Preparation: *Come, Holy Spirit, enlighten the eyes of my heart.* Be present to the God who is always present to you. Call to mind his loving care for you and spend the first minute of your prayer resting in the free, unearned gift of loving and being loved. Let gratitude rise in your heart.

Set the Scene: Ask God for the grace both to experience and to live more deeply your true identity as a beloved child of God.

Read the familiar passage to set the scene. This feast used to be known as the Circumcision of Jesus. The ritual act made a male child a member of the covenant that God had sworn with Abraham (see Gn 17:9–14; 21:4). Medieval writers saw this as the first moment that Jesus shed his precious blood. It confirmed his humanity and his mission as Savior and sacrifice.

LUKE 2:16–21 (LECTIONARY)

The shepherds went in haste to Bethlehem and found Mary and Joseph, and the infant lying in the manger. When they saw this, they made known the message that had been told them about this child. All who heard it were amazed by what had been told them by the shepherds. And Mary kept all these things, reflecting on them in her heart. Then the shepherds returned, glorifying and praising God for all they had heard and seen, just as it had been told to them.

When eight days were completed for his circumcision, he was named Jesus, the name given him by the angel before he was conceived in the womb.

Action! With the calendar reform of the Second Vatican Council, the focus of this feast shifted to Mary, the Mother of God. Read the passage a second time, and this time focus on the Mother of God.

Watch her face respond to the shepherds and the naming and circumcision ceremony. What is going on in her heart? What is she keeping and pondering? Ask her.

Acknowledge: What thoughts, feelings, and desires are rising in your heart?

Relate: Talk to Mary about what is in your heart.

Receive: What does Mary want to tell you about her Son? What does she want to tell you about yourself? What is in Mary's heart for you?

Read the passage a third time.

Respond: Enjoy the company of the Mother of God for a few moments and respond to what she is telling you.

SUGGESTIONS FOR JOURNALING

1. I was surprised by …
2. I had a hard time accepting …
3. My strongest thought, feeling, or desire during this prayer was …
4. I finished prayer wanting …
5. I noticed ________ about Mary, the Mother of God.

After you've journaled, close with a brief conversation with God giving thanks for your prayer experience. Then pray a Hail Mary.

January 2 — Tuesday

Saints Basil and Gregory

These two men were schoolmates, monks, bishops, and close friends. They grew up in Caesarea, Cappadocia (present-day Turkey). Basil became a monk and eventually bishop of his hometown. Gregory preached Basil's funeral in AD 379. He was also a monk and the bishop of Constantinople at a time when the Arian heresy was at its height. Both were famous in their defense of the Trinity against the politically powerful Arians. Gregory followed his friend into eternity in 389.

Preparation: *Come, Holy Spirit, enlighten the eyes of my heart.* Be present to the God who is always present to you. Call to mind his loving care for you and spend the first minute of your prayer resting in the free, unearned gift of loving and being loved. Let gratitude rise in your heart.

Set the Scene: Ask God for the grace both to experience and to live more deeply your true identity as a beloved child of God.

The familiar figure of John the Baptist returns today. Picture him at the banks of the Jordan River. A large crowd has gathered to listen to him preach and receive a baptism of repentance. Well-dressed priests, Levites, and Pharisees approach him wanting to see his "identity card": Who are you? Why are you making a commotion?

Read the passage and picture the scene in your mind.

JOHN 1:19–28 (LECTIONARY)

This is the testimony of John. When the Jews from Jerusalem sent priests and Levites to him to ask him, "Who are you?" he admitted and did not deny it, but admitted, "I am not the Christ." So they asked him, "What are you, then? Are you Elijah?" And he said, "I am not." "Are you the Prophet?" He answered, "No." So they said to him, "Who are you, so we can give an answer to those who sent us? What do you have to say for yourself?" He said: "I am the voice of one crying out in the desert, 'Make

> *straight the way of the Lord,' as Isaiah the prophet said." Some Pharisees were also sent. They asked him, "Why then do you baptize if you are not the Christ or Elijah or the Prophet?" John answered them, "I baptize with water; but there is one among you whom you do not recognize, the one who is coming after me, whose sandal strap I am not worthy to untie." This happened in Bethany across the Jordan, where John was baptizing.*

Action! John the Baptist quotes Isaiah 40:3, a passage we prayed with on December 10, the Second Sunday of Advent. Feel free to flip back to that day and review the Scripture passage and your prayer experience.

Learned Jews would have known much of the Scriptures by memory. John is using Isaiah to tell them that God himself is coming with forgiveness of sins and he will be the Good Shepherd. They seem less than impressed.

Read the passage a second time.

Acknowledge: What stirs in your heart as you picture this scene? How might God be offering you forgiveness of sins and a new life in the New Year?

Relate: Picture Jesus himself somewhere in the crowd witnessing this exchange. He has yet to step forward and reveal himself. Speak to him what is on your heart.

Receive: How does he respond? What does he want to say to you? What is in his heart for you? Read the passage a third time.

Respond: Continue the conversation, then rest with the Lord for a few minutes. Savor his loving presence in your life.

SUGGESTIONS FOR JOURNALING

1. My favorite part of this passage was …
2. When I pictured the scene, I noticed …
3. My strongest thought, feeling, or desire was …

4. Jesus wanted me to know that …
5. I ended prayer wanting …

At the end of your prayer time, spend a minute in gratitude. Thank God for his loving presence in your life. Then pray an Our Father.

January 3 — Wednesday

The Holy Name of Jesus

Mary and Joseph were both instructed by angels to name their child "Jesus" (Lk 1:31, Mt 1:21). It was pronounced Y'shua in his native Aramaic and ΙΗΣΟΥΣ (YE-SOUS) in the Greek language of the New Testament. This is "the name that is above every name, that at the name of Jesus every knee should bend, of those in heaven and on earth and under the earth" (Phil 2:9b–10). St. Bernardine of Siena preached on the Holy Name of Jesus using the monogram IHS (transliterated from the first three letters of Jesus' name in Greek) and added the name of Jesus to the Hail Mary. Today's feast was added to the universal calendar in 1721, dropped in the reform after Vatican II, and brought back by Pope St. John Paul II.

Preparation: *Come, Holy Spirit, enlighten the eyes of my heart.* Be present to the God who is always present to you. Call to mind his loving care for you and spend the first minute of your prayer resting in the free, unearned gift of loving and being loved. Let gratitude rise in your heart.

***Lectio*:** Ask God for the grace both to experience and to live more deeply your true identity as a beloved child of God.

Yesterday the priests, Levites, and Pharisees finished interrogating John and left down the dusty road for Jerusalem. Today, John catches sight of the One for whom he has been preparing the way. Unlike the synoptics, the Gospel of John does not mention Jesus' Baptism. We could imagine that it just happened, and now John the Baptist is excitedly recounting what he saw.

Read the passage and reflect on what these words mean to John and to the world.

JOHN 1:29–34 (LECTIONARY)

John the Baptist saw Jesus coming toward him and said, "Behold, the Lamb of God, who takes away the sin of the world. He is the one of whom I said, 'A man is coming after me who ranks ahead of me because he existed before me.' I did not know him, but the reason why I came baptizing with water was that he might be made known to Israel." John testified further, saying, "I saw the Spirit come down like a dove from the sky and remain upon him. I did not know him, but the one who sent me to baptize with water told me, 'On whomever you see the Spirit come down and remain, he is the one who will baptize with the Holy Spirit.' Now I have seen and testified that he is the Son of God."

***Meditatio*:** Ancient religion was full of sacrifice. They say you could smell the temple before you saw it, an odor that was a mix of slaughterhouse and barbeque. No wonder the temple used so much incense! John identifies Jesus with the Passover lamb, a sacrifice that freed the Israelites from slavery and saved them from death. What does it mean that the Son of God, upon whom the Spirit came down and remained, is also the Lamb of Sacrifice?

Read the passage a second time and notice whatever word or phrase speaks to you.

***Oratio*:** Speak to God what is on your heart. Tell him about the crosses you are carrying, or the search for a sense of purpose. Ask him to share the Holy Spirit with you or to help you know that you, too, are a child of God. Be honest with God.

***Contemplatio*:** Read the passage a third time. Now just receive whatever God wants to give you, especially his loving presence in your life. Be with the Lord for a few minutes.

SUGGESTIONS FOR JOURNALING

1. My favorite word, phrase, or image …
2. I wanted God to know that …
3. God wanted me to know that …
4. How have I personally seen and can testify that Jesus is the Son of God?

At the end of your prayer time, spend a minute in gratitude. Thank God for his loving presence in your life. Then pray an Our Father.

January 4 — Thursday

St. Elizabeth Ann Seton, Religious (USA)

Born in New York in 1774, Elizabeth grew up in the Episcopalian church. At an early age, she learned the value of prayer, Scripture, and the nightly examination of conscience. The belle of New York high society, she married a handsome, wealthy businessman with whom she had five children. His business failed, and he died of tuberculosis, leaving her a penniless widow by the age of thirty. The kindness of friends during her husband's death opened her heart to the Catholic Church. She was drawn by the Eucharist, devotion to Mary, and a conviction that the Catholic Church led back to the apostles and to Jesus. Many friends rejected her when she became Catholic in March 1805. She opened a school, the first American Catholic orphanage, and eventually a religious order. "Mother Seton," as she became known, died on this day in 1821. Her journey had taken her from ordinary goodness to heroic sanctity, and to becoming the first American-born citizen to be canonized.

Preparation: *Come, Holy Spirit, enlighten the eyes of my heart.* Be present to the God who is always present to you. Call to mind his loving care for you and spend the first minute of your prayer resting in the free, unearned gift of loving and being loved. Let gratitude rise in your heart.

***Lectio*:** Ask God for the grace both to experience and to live more deeply your true identity as a beloved child of God.

In his Gospel, Saint John refers to himself as the "disciple whom Jesus loved" (Jn 20:2) and speaks frequently of the depth of God's love. Today, he speaks some hard words about sinners. He is speaking not to tax collectors and prostitutes, but rather to "church people." He wants us to realize that we cannot claim to be righteous if we do not love our brothers. Read the passage slowly and prayerfully.

1 JOHN 3:7–10 (LECTIONARY)

Children, let no one deceive you. The person who acts in righteousness is righteous, just as he is righteous. Whoever sins belongs to the Devil, because the Devil has sinned from the beginning. Indeed, the Son of God was revealed to destroy the works of the Devil. No one who is begotten by God commits sin, because God's seed remains in him; he cannot sin because he is begotten by God. In this way, the children of God and the children of the Devil are made plain; no one who fails to act in righteousness belongs to God, nor anyone who does not love his brother.

Meditatio: Imagine for a moment that you were an orphan living out on the streets. One day, a wealthy business owner takes pity on you and adopts you as his own child. Suddenly you have more than you could ever want. Saint John pictures our adoption by God the Father as a similar dramatic turn of fortune.

Now imagine that despite all that you have received, you continue to live the life of stealing, dishonesty, and running from the law that you learned on the streets. Your new "Daddy" would be deeply grieved. Saint John says that we act in this same way when we fail to love our brothers. Reflect on the undeserved graces you have received, and the ways you have failed to respond to God's generosity.

Read the passage a second time and notice whatever word or phrase speaks to you.

Oratio: Jesus is the true Son of the Father. He shows us how we should act as children of God. Speak to God with gratitude for all his gifts and sorrow for the ways you have failed to live up to your new identity. Don't be afraid to ask for help. Be honest with God; he already knows.

Contemplatio: Read the passage a third time. Listen to God's heart and notice what he wants to give or say to you. Spend a few minutes in his loving presence and savor his deep, abiding, and unconditional mercy.

SUGGESTIONS FOR JOURNALING

1. I was particularly struck by …
2. God wanted me to notice …
3. I am grateful for …
4. I felt convicted that …
5. I feel called to a new way of thinking or acting by …

At the end of your prayer time, spend a minute in gratitude. Thank God for the blessing of this time together. Then pray an Our Father.

January 5 — Friday
Friday Before Epiphany

Preparation: *Come, Holy Spirit, enlighten the eyes of my heart.* Be present to the God who is always present to you. Call to mind his loving care for you and spend the first minute of your prayer resting in the free, unearned gift of loving and being loved. Let gratitude rise in your heart.

***Lectio*:** Ask God for the grace both to experience and to live more deeply your true identity as a beloved child of God.

Cain reappears today. The archetype of sibling rivalry, he was jealous and angry that his brother's sacrifice was received with favor and his was not. God invited him to improve himself, but he decided to eliminate the competition. Saint John warns us that we put ourselves on the same road as Cain when we, too, fail to love our brothers. Read the passage slowly and prayerfully.

1 JOHN 3:11–21 (LECTIONARY)

Beloved: This is the message you have heard from the beginning: we should love one another, unlike Cain who belonged to the Evil One and slaughtered his brother. Why did he slaughter him? Because his own works were evil, and those of his brother righteous. Do not be amazed, then, brothers and sisters, if the world hates you. We know that we have passed from death to life because we love our brothers. Whoever does not love remains in death. Everyone who hates his brother is a murderer, and you know that no murderer has eternal life remaining in him. The way we came to know love was that he laid down his life for us; so we ought to lay down our lives for our brothers. If someone who has worldly means sees a brother in need and refuses him compassion, how can the love of God remain in him? Children, let us love not in word or speech, but in deed and truth.

Now this is how we shall know that we belong to the

truth and reassure our hearts before him in whatever our hearts condemn, for God is greater than our hearts and knows everything. Beloved, if our hearts do not condemn us, we have confidence in God.

***Meditatio*:** God never calls us to anything that he himself is not willing to do. Jesus models true love when he lays down his life for us who are his brothers. Then he calls us to respond in the same way. We don't have to wait for an opportunity to die for another. Even just an act of charity, such as helping a brother in need, will put us on the right track.

Read the passage a second time and notice what thoughts, feelings, or desires move in your heart.

***Oratio*:** Is there anyone in particular you are finding hard to love right now? Jesus not only teaches us how to love, but also helps us to love. Turn to Jesus now and ask him for help. Be honest with God; he already knows.

***Contemplatio*:** Read the passage a third time. Listen to God's heart and notice what he wants to give you or say to you. We cannot give to others what we have not received. Spend a few minutes in his loving presence and savor the deep, abiding, and unconditional love he has for you.

SUGGESTIONS FOR JOURNALING

1. How has Jesus reassured me of his love for me, despite my shortcomings?
2. Whom do I find hard to love right now?
3. Jesus reminded me that …
4. I felt encouraged by …
5. One way I can share God's love with the needy is …

At the end of your prayer time, spend a minute in gratitude. Thank God for the blessing of this time together. Then pray an Our Father.

January 6 — Saturday

The Epiphany of the Lord

The word Epiphany means "manifestation." Jesus is manifest as more than just the King of the Jews, but as the King of all the nations. Saint Matthew saw ancient prophecies being fulfilled by the visit of the Magi, who represent the pagan nations. The liturgical feast of the Epiphany is transferred to Sunday, but there's no reason why we can't also celebrate on its proper day. The Eastern churches refer to this day as "Little Christmas" or "Theophany." Many cultures have special traditions associated with this feast, including parades, special foods, and gift-giving. Bless your home today, or plan ahead for a blessing party tomorrow. Instructions follow the prayer time.

REVIEW

In addition to the review below, or in place of it, you could choose to repeat any one of the meditations from the past week, if you find that to be a fruitful exercise.

Preparation: *Come, Holy Spirit, enlighten the eyes of my heart.* Call to mind God's loving care for you this past week and spend the first minute of your prayer resting in the free, unearned gift of loving and being loved. Let gratitude rise in your heart.

Grace for the Day: What is the desire of your heart? Try to notice what you most deeply desire. Then share it with God in your own words, being confident that he loves you and wants to give you every blessing.

Week in Review: Flip back through your past week's journal entries. As you do, notice what emerged in the conversation. Here are some questions to help you:

1. Where did I notice God, and what was he doing or saying?
2. How did I respond to what God was doing?
3. I felt God's love most strongly when …

4. I found myself struggling with …
5. I'm grateful for …
6. This past week, my strongest sense, image, moment, or experience of God's loving presence was …

Conclude by conversing with God about your week. Acknowledge what you have been experiencing. Relate it to him. Receive what he wants to give you. Respond to him. Then savor that image of God's loving presence and rest there for a minute or two. Close with an Our Father.

Blessing of the Home and Household on Epiphany

The chalking of the doors is a centuries-old practice throughout the world. While less known in the United States, it is becoming more celebrated and is an easy tradition to adopt, dedicating our year to God, asking his blessing on our homes and on all who live, work, or visit us there. Families can be encouraged to bring chalk for a general blessing after Mass on Epiphany to bring home and mark their doors using the following prayer.

The leader should be the head of the household (father, if the father is present). A reader may also be chosen. If one lives alone, the responses are also done by the leader himself, or one might invite friends and neighbors for the celebration. If the home has put out a Christmas crèche, that might be the best place to gather. The letters C, M, and B stand for the traditional names of the Three Wise Men.

The leader makes the Sign of the Cross:

+ In the name of the Father, and of the Son, and of the Holy Spirit.

All reply: Amen.

The leader greets those present in the following words:

Let us praise God, who fills our hearts and homes with peace. Blessed be God forever.

Response: Blessed be God forever.

Leader: The Word became flesh and made his dwelling place among us. It is Christ who enlightens our hearts and homes with his love. May all who enter this home find Christ's light and love.

Reader: Listen to the words of the holy Gospel according to Matthew:

> When Jesus was born in Bethlehem of Judea, in the days of King Herod, behold, magi from the east arrived in Jerusalem, saying, "Where is the newborn king of the Jews? We saw his star at its rising and have come to do him homage." When King Herod heard this, he was greatly troubled, and all Jerusalem with him.
>
> Assembling all the chief priests and the scribes of the people, he inquired of them where the Christ was to be born. They said to him, "In Bethlehem of Judea, for thus it has been written through the prophet:
>
> > *And you, Bethlehem, land of Judah, are by no means least among the rulers of Judah; since from you shall come a ruler, who is to shepherd my people Israel.*"
>
> Then Herod called the magi secretly and ascertained from them the time of the star's appearance. He sent them to Bethlehem and said, "Go and search diligently for the child. When you have found him, bring me word, that I too may go and do him homage." After their audience with the king they set out. And behold, the star that they had seen at its rising preceded them, until it came and stopped over the place where the child was. They were overjoyed at seeing the star, and on entering the house they saw the child with Mary his mother. They prostrated themselves and did him homage. Then they opened their treasures and offered him gifts of gold, frankincense, and myrrh. And having been warned in a dream not to return to Herod, they departed for their country by another way.

The intercessions are then said:

Leader: The Son of God made his home among us. With thanks and praise let us call upon him.
Response: Stay with us, Lord.

Reader: Lord Jesus Christ, with Mary and Joseph you formed the Holy Family: remain in our home, that we may know you as our guest and honor you as our Head. We pray:
Response: Stay with us, Lord.

Reader: Lord Jesus Christ, you had no place to lay your head, but in the spirit of poverty accepted the hospitality of your friends: grant that through our help the homeless may obtain proper housing. We pray:
Response: Stay with us, Lord.

Reader: Lord Jesus Christ, the three kings presented their gifts to you in praise and adoration: grant that those living in this house may use their talents and abilities to your greater glory. We pray:
Response: Stay with us, Lord.

After the intercessions the leader invites all present to say the Lord's Prayer.

The leader then prays the blessing:

Lord God of heaven and earth, you revealed your only-begotten Son to every nation by the guidance of a star. Bless this house and all who inhabit it. Fill us with the light of Christ, that our concern for others may reflect your love. We ask this through Christ our Lord.
Response: Amen.

The leader concludes the rite by signing himself or herself with the sign of the cross and saying: May Christ Jesus dwell with us, + keep us from all harm, and make us one in mind and heart, now and forever.

Response: Amen.

The leader takes the blessed chalk and marks the lintel (the doorframe above the door) on the inside of the main entrance to the house as follows: **20 + C + M + B + 24** (insert the last two digits of the current year).

Other doors may be chalked, for example, the bedroom doors by those who sleep in each room. It is preferable to end the celebration with a suitable song, for example, "O Come, All Ye Faithful" or "We Three Kings." Afterwards the family or host and invited guests might share a meal or a Twelfth Night party, or enjoy a king cake.

—Adapted from USCCB
(https://www.usccb.org/prayers/blessing-home-and-household-epiphany)

Week Six

Keep the Christmas Light Burning Brightly

The traditional American celebration of Christmas begins as early as possible and ends on Christmas Day. In contrast, the Catholic celebration starts on Christmas Day. Officially, the Catholic celebration ends on the feast of the Baptism of the Lord (usually a Sunday, except when Epiphany is transferred forward to January 7 or 8). It seems that our ancestors were fond of making Christmas last for forty days. In medieval and Tudor England, homes would be decorated with greenery such as laurel, holly, ivy, and rosemary at Christmas time. These decorations would remain until Candlemas Eve. Candlemas is the old English name for the feast of the Presentation, celebrated on February 2. This was the day that Jesus was presented in the Temple (see Lk 2:22–40). My first year as a priest, I turned to February 2 in the Roman Missal and was taken aback: The instructions said to begin outside of church with blessing of candles and process into church carrying lit candles. Clearly, this feast used to be a big deal.

I think that we would do well to recover Candlemas as a final Christmas feast. Celebrating Candlemas gives us forty days to savor Christmas. We need the lights and cheer, especially during the dreary days of January. And the waiting of Advent makes more sense when you can savor a longer Christmas.

Even though the liturgical season of Christmas will be over, your own personal celebration can continue. I encourage you to keep your Advent wreath and Nativity scene up in the spirit of the old English tradition. Keep praying and keep savoring the light of Christ shining from the manger scene. God has more to give. Let us keep our hearts open to receive.

Grace of the Week: This week we will return to Ordinary Time. Our readings are drawn from the daily Mass readings. Let us open our hearts to hear Christ calling us to come and follow him. Ask God for the grace to say "Yes" each day to his voice calling us.

Announcement of Easter and the Moveable Feasts for the year 2024

The following text is traditionally read or chanted after the Gospel of Epiphany. It reminds us of the days before Google when you couldn't simply ask your smartphone when Easter is. It also reminds us that the mystery of God's love for us is not exhausted at Christmas. Like the old television shows, we are told: "Stay tuned!"

> *Know, dear brethren (brothers and sisters), that, as we have rejoiced at the Nativity of our Lord Jesus Christ, so by leave of God's mercy we announce to you also the joy of his Resurrection, who is our Savior.*
>
> *On the fourteenth day of February will fall Ash Wednesday, and the beginning of the fast of the most sacred Lenten season.*
>
> *On the thirty-first day of March you will celebrate with joy Easter Day, the Paschal feast of our Lord Jesus Christ.*
>
> *On the ninth day of May will be the Ascension of our Lord Jesus Christ. (Or the twelfth day of May where the Ascension is transferred to Sunday)*
>
> *On the nineteenth day of May, the feast of Pentecost.*
>
> *On the thirtieth day of May, the feast of the Most Holy Body and Blood of Christ. (Or the second day of June where Corpus Christi is transferred to Sunday)*
>
> *On the first day of December, the First Sunday of the Advent of our Lord Jesus Christ, to whom is honor and glory for ever and ever. Amen.*

January 7 — Sunday

Epiphany of the Lord (Observed)

"The *Epiphany* is the manifestation of Jesus as Messiah of Israel, Son of God and Savior of the world. The great feast of Epiphany celebrates the adoration of Jesus by the wise men (*magi*) from the East, together with his baptism in the Jordan and the wedding feast at Cana in Galilee. In the magi, representatives of the neighboring pagan religions, the Gospel sees the first-fruits of the nations, who welcome the good news of salvation through the Incarnation. The magi's coming to Jerusalem in order to pay homage to the king of the Jews shows that they seek in Israel, in the messianic light of the star of David, the one who will be king of the nations. Their coming means that pagans can discover Jesus and worship him as Son of God and Savior of the world only by turning towards the Jews and receiving from them the messianic promise as contained in the Old Testament. The Epiphany shows that 'the full number of the nations' now takes its 'place in the family of the patriarchs,' and acquires *Israelitica dignitas* ('the dignity of Israel's birthright')" (CCC 528).

Preparation: *Come, Holy Spirit, enlighten the eyes of my heart.* Be present to the God who is always present to you. Call to mind his loving care for you and spend the first minute of your prayer resting in the free, unearned gift of loving and being loved. Let gratitude rise in your heart.

Set the Scene: Read through this passage and spend some time really setting the scene. What is the city like? What do the magi look like? Picture the camels threading their way through the streets of Jerusalem, then Bethlehem. What happens when they arrive at "the place where the child was"?

MATTHEW 2:1–12 (LECTIONARY)

When Jesus was born in Bethlehem of Judea, in the days of King Herod, behold, magi from the east arrived in Jerusalem, saying, "Where is the newborn king of the Jews?

We saw his star at its rising and have come to do him homage." When King Herod heard this, he was greatly troubled, and all Jerusalem with him. Assembling all the chief priests and the scribes of the people, he inquired of them where the Christ was to be born. They said to him, "In Bethlehem of Judea, for thus it has been written through the prophet:

> And you, Bethlehem, land of Judah,
> are by no means least among the rulers of Judah;
> since from you shall come a ruler,
> who is to shepherd my people Israel."

Then Herod called the magi secretly and ascertained from them the time of the star's appearance. He sent them to Bethlehem and said, "Go and search diligently for the child. When you have found him, bring me word, that I too may go and do him homage." After their audience with the king they set out. And behold, the star that they had seen at its rising preceded them, until it came and stopped over the place where the child was. They were overjoyed at seeing the star, and on entering the house they saw the child with Mary his mother. They prostrated themselves and did him homage. Then they opened their treasures and offered him gifts of gold, frankincense, and myrrh. And having been warned in a dream not to return to Herod, they departed for their country by another way.

Action! Play the scene forward in your mind. The magi have made quite the pilgrimage. What was it like? Did they experience frustration? How did they encourage each other? What goes through their minds and hearts as they finally arrive?

They find the child with his mother. Picture the relationship between Mary and Jesus. What thoughts or feelings are in Mary's heart? The hearts of the wise men? The heart of the infant Christ?

Acknowledge: Read the passage a second time. You, too, have been on a long pilgrimage. What thoughts, feelings, and desires rise in your heart?

Relate: Share your thoughts and feelings with Mary, the Mother of God. How does she respond to you?

Read the passage a third time, or just the part that speaks to you.

Receive: What does she want to tell you about her son? What does she want to tell you about yourself? What is in Mary's heart for you?

Respond: You have a gift to give. Open your treasures and respond by giving the Christ Child your gift.

SUGGESTIONS FOR JOURNALING

1. The part of the passage that most spoke to me was…
2. I was particularly moved by …
3. The gift I want to give Jesus is …
4. The gift that Jesus and Mary had for me was …
5. How were the magi changed by their experience?
6. How have I been changed by this journey?

After you've journaled, close with a brief conversation with God giving thanks for your prayer experience. Then pray an Our Father.

January 8 — Monday
Baptism of the Lord

This feast marks the end of the liturgical Christmas season and the beginning of Ordinary Time. It is always celebrated on the Sunday after Epiphany, except in the years when Epiphany is transferred forward to January 7 or 8. In that case the feast of the Baptism is celebrated on the Monday following.

Preparation: *Come, Holy Spirit, enlighten the eyes of my heart.* Be present to the God who is always present to you. Call to mind his loving care for you and spend the first minute of your prayer resting in the free, unearned gift of loving and being loved. Let gratitude rise in your heart.

Set the Scene: Ask God for the grace to say "yes" to his voice each day.

John the Baptist is living in the wilderness. He eats locusts and wild honey and wears a cloak of camel's hair with a leather belt around his waist. People are thronging to him to confess their sins and be baptized. Read the passage and use your imagination to set the scene.

MARK 1:7–11 (LECTIONARY)

This is what he proclaimed: "One mightier than I is coming after me. I am not worthy to stoop and loosen the thongs of his sandals. I have baptized you with water; he will baptize you with the Holy Spirit."

It happened in those days that Jesus came from Nazareth of Galilee and was baptized in the Jordan by John. On coming up out of the water he saw the heavens being torn open and the Spirit, like a dove, descending upon him. And a voice came from the heavens, "You are my beloved Son; with you I am well pleased."

Action! Play the scene forward in your mind. Jesus appears first in a humble way, blending in with the mass of sinners on their way to baptism. Picture our Savior entering the waters of baptism. What does Jesus look like? What does he see? How does Jesus feel?

Acknowledge: Read the passage a second time. Put yourself in the scene. What are you longing for or worried about as you hear John proclaiming, "One mightier than I"? What is in your heart as you rub shoulders with Jesus on the way to baptism? What does this passage stir up within you?

Relate: As the Scripture scene comes to a close, Jesus emerges from the water. Go over and talk to Jesus. Share with him what is on your heart.

Receive: How does Jesus respond? What does he want to say to you or give you? Be open to whatever God is offering: a word, thought, or feeling.

Respond: Continue the conversation for a little while. Then just rest in the love God has for you, the same love that the Father has for his only-begotten Son.

SUGGESTIONS FOR JOURNALING

1. I was surprised by …
2. I was especially moved by …
3. I sensed God was with me and wanted me to know …
4. I ended prayer wanting …

After you've journaled, close with a brief conversation with God about your prayer experience. Then pray an Our Father.

January 9 — Tuesday

Tuesday of the First Week in Ordinary Time

Preparation: *Come, Holy Spirit, enlighten the eyes of my heart.* Be present to the God who is always present to you. Call to mind his loving care for you and spend the first minute of your prayer resting in the free, unearned gift of loving and being loved. Let gratitude rise in your heart.

Set the Scene: My final year in seminary, I had the privilege of making a pilgrimage to the Holy Land. We spent some time in the ruins of the city of Capernaum. This city sat right on the shore of the lake. The fishermen probably disembarked on a wharf or on the beach just out of town. Jesus called his disciples first, and they followed him before anything amazing had happened. He led them to the local synagogue on the Sabbath, where he had an important message for all the people to hear.

Read the passage and focus your imagination on the early first-century place of worship.

MARK 1:14–28 (LECTIONARY)

After John had been arrested, Jesus came to Galilee proclaiming the Gospel of God: "This is the time of fulfillment. The Kingdom of God is at hand. Repent, and believe in the Gospel."

As he passed by the Sea of Galilee, he saw Simon and his brother Andrew casting their nets into the sea; they were fishermen. Jesus said to them, "Come after me, and I will make you fishers of men." Then they left their nets and followed him. He walked along a little farther and saw James, the son of Zebedee, and his brother John. They too were in a boat mending their nets. Then he called them. So they left their father Zebedee in the boat along with the hired men and followed him.

Jesus came to Capernaum with his followers, and on

> *the sabbath he entered the synagogue and taught. The people were astonished at his teaching, for he taught them as one having authority and not as the scribes. In their synagogue was a man with an unclean spirit; he cried out, "What have you to do with us, Jesus of Nazareth? Have you come to destroy us? I know who you are — the Holy One of God!" Jesus rebuked him and said, "Quiet! Come out of him!" The unclean spirit convulsed him and with a loud cry came out of him. All were amazed and asked one another, "What is this? A new teaching with authority. He commands even the unclean spirits and they obey him." His fame spread everywhere throughout the whole region of Galilee.*

Action! The people are amazed less at what Jesus says and more at how he says it. He preaches with authority. Then something amazing happens — a possessed man begins shouting at the preacher. The preacher addresses the man and suddenly everyone is witnessing an exorcism. How do the people respond? Find yourself in the scene — are you among Jesus' disciples, or are you somewhere in the crowd?

Acknowledge: Read the passage again. What part strikes you? What does this passage stir up in your heart — what thoughts, desires, hopes, fears?

Relate: After the crowd disperses, go find Jesus. Sit down and talk to him about what you saw and thought and felt. Read the passage a third time as though reviewing it in your mind. Can you see the day's events through Jesus' eyes?

Receive: How does Jesus respond to the things you are sharing? Be open to receive whatever Jesus is offering: a word, thought, or feeling.

Respond: Continue the conversation for a little while. Then rest in the love Jesus has for you, the love that never ceases to amaze us.

SUGGESTIONS FOR JOURNALING

1. If an exorcism happened while I was sitting in church on Sunday, I would …
2. The part that struck me was …
3. My strongest thought, feeling, or desire was …
4. Jesus wanted me to know …
5. Is there a spirit within me, or around me, that opposes the work of the Gospel? Perhaps say, "In the name of Jesus I rebuke the spirit of … (fear, hopelessness, anger, lust, pride, etc.) and I send it to the foot of the cross there to be dealt with by Jesus."

After you've journaled, close with a brief conversation with God the Father giving thanks for your prayer experience. Then pray one Our Father.

January 10 — Wednesday

Wednesday of the First Week in Ordinary Time

Preparation: *Come, Holy Spirit, enlighten the eyes of my heart.* Be present to the God who is always present to you. Call to mind his loving care for you and spend the first minute of your prayer resting in the free, unearned gift of loving and being loved. Let gratitude rise in your heart.

Set the Scene: Ask God for the grace to hear Jesus calling you and to respond with a "yes."

The synagogue is toward the middle of Capernaum. The place identified as Simon's house sits just a few blocks away, down the road between the synagogue and the lake. After their Sabbath worship is over, Jesus and a few of his friends went to Simon's house for a little Sabbath brunch. Picture the scene in your mind.

MARK 1:29–39 (LECTIONARY)

On leaving the synagogue Jesus entered the house of Simon and Andrew with James and John. Simon's mother-in-law lay sick with a fever. They immediately told him about her. He approached, grasped her hand, and helped her up. Then the fever left her and she waited on them.

When it was evening, after sunset, they brought to him all who were ill or possessed by demons. The whole town was gathered at the door. He cured many who were sick with various diseases, and he drove out many demons, not permitting them to speak because they knew him.

Rising very early before dawn, he left and went off to a deserted place, where he prayed. Simon and those who were with him pursued him and on finding him said, "Everyone is looking for you." He told them, "Let us go on to the nearby villages that I may preach there also. For this purpose have I come." So he went into their synagogues, preaching and driving out demons throughout the whole of Galilee.

Action! People were restricted from traveling, working, or going to the doctor on the Sabbath, which ended at sunset. What were they thinking during the day? Let yourself be one of "those who were with" Simon.

Acknowledge: Read the passage a second time. What does it feel like to hear a knock on the door and to look out and see every sick person in town gathered at the door? What do you think or feel as you watch many miracles taking place before your very eyes?

Relate: The passage ends with Jesus heading out on a preaching mission to all the surrounding towns. Walk with Jesus. Tell him what you are thinking and feeling. Read the passage a third time.

Receive: After Jesus has listened to you, be silent and receive. What is in his heart for you?

Respond: Continue the conversation for a little while. Then rest in the love Jesus has for you, the love you find when you go to a deserted place to pray.

SUGGESTIONS FOR JOURNALING

1. My favorite part of today's prayer was …
2. I was not expecting …
3. Today I saw in Jesus …
4. Today Jesus saw in me …
5. I found myself wanting more …

After you've journaled, close with a brief conversation with God giving thanks for your prayer experience. Then pray the Our Father.

January 11 — Thursday

Thursday of the First Week in Ordinary Time

Preparation: *Come, Holy Spirit, enlighten the eyes of my heart.* Be present to the God who is always present to you. Call to mind his loving care for you and spend the first minute of your prayer resting in the free, unearned gift of loving and being loved. Let gratitude rise in your heart.

Set the Scene: Ask God for the grace to say "yes" to his voice each day.

In these early stages of the Gospel proclamation, Jesus does not want people talking about him. But later, after he rises from the dead, he will command his disciples to tell the whole world. Perhaps they have to experience more than just a cure before they are qualified to proclaim the Good News.

As you read the passage, don't focus on Jesus' warning but on his relationship with this leper. Picture the scene in your mind.

MARK 1:40–45 (LECTIONARY)

A leper came to him and kneeling down begged him and said, "If you wish, you can make me clean." Moved with pity, he stretched out his hand, touched the leper, and said to him, "I do will it. Be made clean." The leprosy left him immediately, and he was made clean. Then, warning him sternly, he dismissed him at once. Then he said to him, "See that you tell no one anything, but go, show yourself to the priest and offer for your cleansing what Moses prescribed; that will be proof for them." The man went away and began to publicize the whole matter. He spread the report abroad so that it was impossible for Jesus to enter a town openly. He remained outside in deserted places, and people kept coming to him from everywhere.

Action! Play the scene forward in your mind. How does the leper look at

Jesus? How does Jesus look at the leper? People were forbidden to touch lepers so they wouldn't catch leprosy. What does it feel like to be touched by Jesus?

Acknowledge: Read the passage a second time. Where do you feel unclean? Is there an area of your life that makes you feel ashamed, unwelcome, or afraid to share with others?

Relate: "If you wish, you can make me clean." Share your struggle, your shame, your fear, with Jesus. Let him see what hurts.

Read the passage a third time and picture yourself as the leper.

Receive: Let Jesus touch you where it hurts. What does the touch feel like? Are you afraid, relieved? Does healing happen? Does nothing happen? Do you want to run away?

Respond: Notice what Jesus wants and what you want. Know that Jesus loves you no matter how you feel, and no matter how you receive, or don't receive, what he is offering you.

SUGGESTIONS FOR JOURNALING

1. Jesus wanted me to know …
2. I was afraid that …
3. I was comforted by the realization that …
4. Today Jesus gave me …
5. Who else needs to feel the healing touch of Jesus? Offer a prayer for that person or persons.

After you've journaled, close with a brief conversation with God giving thanks for your prayer experience. Then pray an Our Father.

January 12 — Friday
Friday of the First Week in Ordinary Time

Preparation: *Come, Holy Spirit, enlighten the eyes of my heart.* Be present to the God who is always present to you. Call to mind his loving care for you and spend the first minute of your prayer resting in the free, unearned gift of loving and being loved. Let gratitude rise in your heart.

Set the Scene: Jesus and company have spent some time traveling around the local towns, preaching and healing. Now they have come back to the city of Capernaum. The excitement is so great you can't even get near the house where Jesus is. Some plucky fellows are so determined to get their friend to Jesus that they climb up to the second floor and pull apart the thatched roof. Picture the scene in your mind as you prayerfully read this passage.

MARK 2:1–12 (LECTIONARY)

When Jesus returned to Capernaum after some days, it became known that he was at home. Many gathered together so that there was no longer room for them, not even around the door, and he preached the word to them. They came bringing to him a paralytic carried by four men. Unable to get near Jesus because of the crowd, they opened up the roof above him. After they had broken through, they let down the mat on which the paralytic was lying. When Jesus saw their faith, he said to him, "Child, your sins are forgiven." Now some of the scribes were sitting there asking themselves, "Why does this man speak that way? He is blaspheming. Who but God alone can forgive sins?" Jesus immediately knew in his mind what they were thinking to themselves, so he said, "Why are you thinking such things in your hearts? Which is easier, to say to the paralytic, 'Your sins are forgiven,' or to say, 'Rise, pick up your mat and walk'? But that you may know that the Son of Man has authority to forgive sins on earth" — he said to the paralytic, "I say to you, rise, pick up your mat, and go home." He rose, picked up his mat at once, and went away in the sight of everyone. They were all astounded and glorified God, saying, "We have never seen anything like this."

Action! Play the scene forward in your mind. Where are you in the scene? Are you part of Jesus' company, an excited bystander, or a skeptical scribe? Are you on the roof, bringing a friend to Jesus?

Acknowledge: Read the passage a second time. Sin destroys our relationship with God. It leads to spiritual paralysis and death. When have you felt paralyzed, powerless to move toward God? What are the thoughts, feelings, and desires that rise in your heart?

Relate: Jesus is here for you. He knows your name, even in a crowd. Spend a little time in conversation with him about this scene. Then read the passage a third time.

Receive: What does Jesus want to say, do, or give you? Receive it with joy.

Respond: Continue the conversation. Enter more deeply into a relationship with Jesus, a friendship where you can be together and you don't have to say anything at all.

SUGGESTIONS FOR JOURNALING

1. My favorite part about today's passage was …
2. I struggled with …
3. For me, the crowd that keeps me from Jesus is …
4. Was there someone who brought me to Jesus, when I couldn't bring myself?
5. Was there someone I brought to Jesus, or is there someone I want to bring to Jesus now?

After you've journaled, close with a brief conversation with God giving thanks for your prayer experience. Then pray an Our Father.

January 13 — Saturday

Saturday of the First Week in Ordinary Time

REVIEW

In addition to the review below, or in place of it, you could choose to repeat any one of the meditations from the past week, if you find that to be a fruitful exercise.

Preparation: *Come, Holy Spirit, enlighten the eyes of my heart.* Call to mind God's loving care for you and spend the first minute of your prayer resting in the free, unearned gift of loving and being loved. Let gratitude rise in your heart.

Grace for the Day: What is the desire of your heart? Try to notice what you most deeply desire. Then share it with God in your own words, being confident that he loves you and wants to give you every blessing.

Week in Review: We have just spent a week with Jesus' first disciples. We have watched him teach, cast out demons, work miracles, forgive sins, and draw huge crowds. God has delivered on his promise to send a Savior. Flip back through your past week's journal entries. As you do, notice what emerged in the conversation. Here are some questions to help you:

1. Where did I notice God, and what was he calling me to?
2. How did I respond to what God was doing?
3. I felt God's love most strongly when …
4. I found myself struggling with …
5. I'm grateful for …
6. This past week, my strongest sense, image, moment, or experience of God's loving presence was …

Conclude by conversing with God about your week. Acknowledge what you have been experiencing. Relate it to him. Receive what he wants to give you. Respond to him. Then savor the image of God's loving presence and rest there for a minute or two. Close with an Our Father.

Week Seven

Relational Prayer (ARRR)

I want to teach you a third prayer form, called relational prayer or "A-R-R-R." You've already seen this prayer form as part of imaginative prayer. Let's review the four steps:

> **Acknowledge** what is going on inside of you — your thoughts, feelings, and desires.
>
> **Relate** or share with the Lord what is going on inside of you.
>
> **Receive** what God wants to give you.
>
> **Respond** to what the Lord just gave you.

This prayer form is an excellent way of praying with the experiences of everyday life. Let's say I just hung up the phone after a frustrating call from a difficult person. The conversation infuriated me, and I want to vent about it. Perhaps I suddenly feel the urge to eat a bowl of ice cream (a numbing behavior) or distract myself with TikTok videos. Instead of doing those things, I can turn to Jesus.

First, I need to understand what is going on inside of me. I take a moment to listen to my heart. Why did I get angry? I notice the feelings that happened before I got angry, such as feeling unappreciated, disrespected, or not valued. I might realize I have a wound in this area that makes these kinds of conversations hurt more than they should. I might also be mad at myself for losing my temper or I might be experiencing guilt and shame, or a need to justify myself. I **Acknowledge** those feelings.

Then I turn to Jesus. I could also speak to God the Father, the Holy Spirit, or Mother Mary. It might help to call to mind a favorite image such as the Good Shepherd, Divine Mercy, or one of the memorable moments when Jesus and I connected through imaginative prayer. I could picture my prayer space at home or a favorite adoration chapel and imagine I am there.

Next, I share my heart with him — I **Relate** what is going on. The important thing here is that my focus needs to shift from me and my problem to the Lord. First, it was me looking at my problem; then, both of us looking at my problem; now, I'm looking at him.

Then, I **Receive** what he wants to give me: a feeling, a thought, a reminder, a Scripture passage, etc. I also might realize things, like I tend to be a people-pleaser or I was frustrated before the conversation started.

Finally, I **Respond** by acting according to this new vision. I might do this by letting go of something, or resolving to handle things differently next time with Jesus' help. Perhaps, I need to pray for the other person or forgive them. I might need to forgive myself. I end with gratitude to God.

Try it for yourself at some point this week. You will be surprised how much this simple prayer form will change your life. Sharing your burdens with God makes them shrink like snow in the sunshine.

Grace of the Week: John the Baptist was the first person to call Jesus "the Lamb of God" (Jn 1:29). We will delve into some of the Scriptures that flesh out the meaning of this term. Pray for the grace to more deeply appreciate the Lamb of God who lays down his precious life for you.

January 14 — Sunday

Second Sunday in Ordinary Time

Preparation: *Come, Holy Spirit, enlighten the eyes of my heart.* Be present to the God who is always present to you. Call to mind his loving care for you and spend the first minute of your prayer resting in the free, unearned gift of loving and being loved. Let gratitude rise in your heart.

Set the Scene: Ask God for the grace to more deeply appreciate the Lamb of God, who lays down his precious life for you. John is not the Messiah but has been preparing the way for one greater than himself. His disciples are full of expectation. Picture the wilderness scene again. Where is Jesus staying? Use your imagination as you read this passage prayerfully.

JOHN 1:35–42 (LECTIONARY)

John was standing with two of his disciples, and as he watched Jesus walk by, he said, "Behold, the Lamb of God." The two disciples heard what he said and followed Jesus. Jesus turned and saw them following him and said to them, "What are you looking for?" They said to him, "Rabbi" — which translated means Teacher —, "where are you staying?" He said to them, "Come, and you will see." So they went and saw where he was staying, and they stayed with him that day. It was about four in the afternoon. Andrew, the brother of Simon Peter, was one of the two who heard John and followed Jesus. He first found his own brother Simon and told him, "We have found the Messiah" — which is translated Christ —. Then he brought him to Jesus. Jesus looked at him and said, "You are Simon the son of John; you will be called Cephas" — which is translated Peter.

Action! Play the scene forward in your mind. This moment was so life-changing that John (the beloved disciple) even remembers the hour of the day when he first met Jesus. What is going on inside the hearts of the disciples? What do they see in Jesus? What does Jesus see when he looks at Simon?

Acknowledge: Read the passage a second time. What does this passage stir up in your heart — what thoughts, desires, hopes, fears? What do you see when you look at Jesus? What does Jesus see when he looks at you?

Relate: Have a conversation with Jesus. "What are you looking for?" Share with him what is on your heart.

Receive: Read the passage a third time. How does Jesus respond? What does he want to say to you or give you? Be open to whatever God is offering.

Respond: After a little conversation, let yourself stay with the Lord for a while.

SUGGESTIONS FOR JOURNALING

1. I was not expecting …
2. I was especially moved by …
3. When Jesus looks at me …
4. I ended prayer wanting …
5. The person I most want to introduce to Jesus is …

After you've journaled, close with a brief conversation with God giving thanks for your prayer experience. Then pray an Our Father.

January 15 — Monday

Monday of the Second Week in Ordinary Time

Preparation: *Come, Holy Spirit, enlighten the eyes of my heart.* Be present to the God who is always present to you. Call to mind his loving care for you and spend the first minute of your prayer resting in the free, unearned gift of loving and being loved. Let gratitude rise in your heart.

Set the Scene: As we explore the theme of the Lamb of God in Scripture, we begin with a very difficult scene from the Old Testament. God instructs Abraham to sacrifice his only son. This practice seems unthinkable to us, but it was fairly common in the ancient world. In the city of Carthage, which was larger than Athens and for many years more important than Rome, it was common to sacrifice infant children as a ritual offering to the gods. God has an important lesson for Abraham and Isaac. Read the passage slowly and prayerfully.

GENESIS 22:1–14

God put Abraham to the test and said to him: Abraham! "Here I am!" he replied. Then God said: Take your son Isaac, your only one, whom you love, and go to the land of Moriah. There offer him up as a burnt offering on one of the heights that I will point out to you. Early the next morning Abraham saddled his donkey, took with him two of his servants and his son Isaac, and after cutting the wood for the burnt offering, set out for the place of which God had told him.

On the third day Abraham caught sight of the place from a distance. Abraham said to his servants: "Stay here with the donkey, while the boy and I go on over there. We will worship and then come back to you." So Abraham took the wood for the burnt offering and laid it on his son Isaac, while he himself carried the fire and the knife. As the two walked on together, Isaac spoke to his father Abraham. "Father!" he said. "Here I am," he replied. Isaac continued, "Here are the fire and the wood, but where is the sheep for the burnt offering?" "My son," Abraham answered, "God will provide the sheep for the burnt offering." Then the two walked on together.

When they came to the place of which God had told him, Abraham built an altar there and arranged the wood on it. Next he bound his son Isaac, and put him on top of the wood on the altar. Then Abraham reached out and took the knife to slaughter his son. But the angel of the LORD called to him from heaven, "Abraham, Abraham!" "Here I am," he answered. "Do not lay your hand on the boy," said the angel. "Do not do the least thing to him. For now I know that you fear God, since you did not withhold from me your son, your only one." Abraham looked up and saw a single ram caught by its horns in the thicket. So Abraham went and took the ram and offered it up as a burnt offering in place of his son. Abraham named that place Yahweh-yireh; hence people today say, "On the mountain the LORD will provide."

Action! Play the scene forward in your mind. What is going on inside Abraham? How about Isaac? What stands out to you?

Acknowledge: Read the passage a second time. This time listen to your heart. What thoughts and feelings are you experiencing as you imagine this gut-wrenching scene?

Relate: God loves every child like an only child. He loves you even more than Abraham loved Isaac. Have a conversation with God. Share with him what is on your heart.

Receive: Read the passage a third time. How does God the Father respond to you? "God will provide the sheep for the burnt offering." God stops the hand of Abraham, because he will send Jesus, his only Son whom he loves, to take Isaac's place. Jesus will carry the wood up the mountain and become the sacrifice. How did the Father feel when his Son was led like a lamb to the slaughter and opened not his mouth? Receive the Father's love for Jesus, and for you.

Respond: Rest in the love of God for a little while. You are safe with him.

SUGGESTIONS FOR JOURNALING

1. I had never noticed before …
2. What really struck me was …
3. I see more clearly that …
4. My heart breaks when …
5. My deepest desire is …

After you've journaled, close with a brief conversation with God giving thanks for your prayer experience. Then pray an Our Father.

January 16 — Tuesday

Tuesday of the Second Week in Ordinary Time

Preparation: *Come, Holy Spirit, enlighten the eyes of my heart.* Be present to the God who is always present to you. Call to mind his loving care for you and spend the first minute of your prayer resting in the free, unearned gift of loving and being loved. Let gratitude rise in your heart.

Set the Scene: Ask God for the grace to more deeply appreciate the Lamb of God, who lays down his precious life for you. We move down the timeline to the descendants of Abraham. God had saved them from a severe famine by saving Joseph, Abraham's great-grandson, from his jealous brothers and making him a high-ranking official in Egypt (see Gn 37, 39–47). The Israelites grew so numerous that the Egyptians feared and then enslaved them. God sends Moses to set them free by afflicting the Egyptians with terrible plagues. Nine plagues have already visited Egypt and now this tenth will be the worst of all: the death of the firstborn. Moses is given careful instructions for what the Israelites must do to escape the plague. Read the passage slowly and prayerfully.

EXODUS 12:1–13

The LORD said to Moses and Aaron in the land of Egypt: This month will stand at the head of your calendar; you will reckon it the first month of the year. Tell the whole community of Israel: On the tenth of this month every family must procure for itself a lamb, one apiece for each household. If a household is too small for a lamb, it along with its nearest neighbor will procure one, and apportion the lamb's cost in proportion to the number of persons, according to what each household consumes. Your lamb must be a year-old male and without blemish. You may take it from either the sheep or the goats. You will keep it until the fourteenth day of this month, and then, with the whole community of Israel assembled, it will be slaughtered during the evening twilight. They will take some of its blood and apply it to the two doorposts and the lintel of the houses in which they eat it. They will consume its meat that same night, eating it roasted with unleavened bread and bitter herbs. Do not eat any of it raw or even boiled in water, but roasted, with its head and shanks and inner organs. You must not keep any of it beyond the morning; whatever is left over in the morning must be burned up.

This is how you are to eat it: with your loins girt, sandals on your feet and your staff in hand, you will eat it in a hurry. It is the LORD's Passover. For on this same night I will go through Egypt, striking down every firstborn in the land, human being and beast alike, and executing judgment on all the gods of Egypt — I, the LORD! But for you the blood will mark the houses where you are. Seeing the blood, I will pass over you; thereby, when I strike the land of Egypt, no destructive blow will come upon you.

Action! Play the scene forward in your mind. Picture the people following God's instructions: killing the lamb, painting the blood, and eating the roasted flesh with unleavened bread and bitter herbs. What would that night have felt like?

Acknowledge: Place yourself among the Chosen People. You grew up in Egypt enduring the abuse of the Egyptians. What are you experiencing this night? Read the passage a second time.

Relate: Have a conversation with God. Share with him what is on your heart. What kind of slavery have you experienced? When have you been a victim of abuse? Do you believe that God will set you free? Talk to the Father about everything.

Receive: Read the passage a third time. How does God the Father respond to you? In what way does he want to set you free?

Respond: The Passover ritual will one day form the basis of the Last Supper and the far greater gift of the Eucharist. God's Chosen People will gather weekly to eat the flesh of the Lamb of God and drink his blood. "What wondrous love is this, O my soul?" Spend a few moments receiving and savoring the love of the Father, Son, and Holy Spirit.

SUGGESTIONS FOR JOURNALING

1. The part that most spoke to me was …
2. My heart hurt when I realized …
3. I found comfort in …
4. God wants to set me free from …
5. I am afraid that …

After you've journaled, close with a brief conversation with God giving thanks for your prayer experience. Then pray an Our Father.

January 17 — Wednesday

Wednesday of the Second Week in Ordinary Time

SAINT ANTHONY, ABBOT

Anthony was born in Egypt around AD 251. At the age of eighteen or so, he was in a church and heard the Bible passage, "Go, sell what you have, and give to [the] poor, and you will have treasure in heaven; then come, follow me" (Mk 10:21). Anthony believed this was a personal invitation from God directed to him. He gave away his earthly possessions and went out into the desert to live a simple life of prayer and penance. During this period, the Church transitioned from persecuted minority to a kind of state religion. Christianity became too easy and comfortable for the likes of many. Many who desired to give their all for Jesus went out into the desert and joined Anthony. He wrote a rule for them which became the foundations of the monastic life.

What message does God have for you in today's Scripture passage?

Preparation: *Come, Holy Spirit, enlighten the eyes of my heart.* Be present to the God who is always present to you. Call to mind his loving care for you and spend the first minute of your prayer resting in the free, unearned gift of loving and being loved. Let gratitude rise in your heart.

***Lectio*:** Ask God for the grace to more deeply appreciate the Lamb of God, who lays down his precious life for you. We move forward in time to the Suffering Servant passages from Isaiah. Our reading today is long but full of rich imagery. Read the passage slowly and prayerfully.

ISAIAH 53:1–12

Who would believe what we have heard?
To whom has the arm of the LORD been revealed?
He grew up like a sapling before him,
like a shoot from the parched earth;
He had no majestic bearing to catch our eye,

no beauty to draw us to him.
He was spurned and avoided by men,
a man of suffering, knowing pain,
Like one from whom you turn your face,
spurned, and we held him in no esteem.

Yet it was our pain that he bore,
our sufferings he endured.
We thought of him as stricken,
struck down by God and afflicted,
But he was pierced for our sins,
crushed for our iniquity.
He bore the punishment that makes us whole,
by his wounds we were healed.
We had all gone astray like sheep,
all following our own way;
But the LORD laid upon him
the guilt of us all.

Though harshly treated, he submitted
and did not open his mouth;
Like a lamb led to slaughter
or a sheep silent before shearers,
he did not open his mouth.
Seized and condemned, he was taken away.
Who would have thought any more of his destiny?
For he was cut off from the land of the living,
struck for the sins of his people.
He was given a grave among the wicked,
a burial place with evildoers,
Though he had done no wrong,
nor was deceit found in his mouth.
But it was the LORD's will to crush him with pain.
By making his life as a reparation offering,
he shall see his offspring, shall lengthen his days,
and the LORD's will shall be accomplished through him.

Because of his anguish he shall see the light;
because of his knowledge he shall be content;
My servant, the just one, shall justify the many,
their iniquity he shall bear.
Therefore I will give him his portion among the many,
and he shall divide the spoils with the mighty,
Because he surrendered himself to death,
was counted among the transgressors,
Bore the sins of many,
and interceded for the transgressors.

***Meditatio*:** Was there a particular word, phrase, or idea that spoke to you? What does it stir in your heart?

Read the passage again, pausing to reflect on whatever stands out to you. Focus on the part that speaks most to you.

***Oratio*:** This man's life is a sacrifice, poured out for others. Though he endures many bitter agonies, they are worth it. His stripes heal us, and God rewards him for being a faithful servant. As you read this passage a third time, speak to God what is in your heart — your thoughts, feelings, and desires.

***Contemplatio*:** Open your heart to receive what God wants to give you. Jesus endured the cross because he loves you and wants to make you whole. How does God want you to experience love and wholeness today? Spend some time just receiving God's love and resting in it.

SUGGESTIONS FOR JOURNALING

1. The heaviest part for me was …
2. I see Jesus' sufferings in a new light …
3. I was really struck by …
4. I had a hard time accepting …
5. I ended prayer feeling …

After you've journaled, close with a brief conversation with God about your prayer experience. Then pray an Our Father.

January 18 — Thursday

Thursday of the Second Week in Ordinary Time

Preparation: *Come, Holy Spirit, enlighten the eyes of my heart.* Be present to the God who is always present to you. Call to mind his loving care for you and spend the first minute of your prayer resting in the free, unearned gift of loving and being loved. Let gratitude rise in your heart.

Set the Scene: Ask God for the grace to more deeply appreciate the Lamb of God, who lays down his precious life for you. For centuries, the Israelites gathered to celebrate the Passover with unleavened bread, the meat of a sacrificial lamb, and four symbolic cups of wine. They could not have known that God had commanded this special meal as a precursor to the Mass and the Most Blessed Sacrament. Picture the scene in your mind as you read this passage.

MARK 14:12–25

On the first day of the Feast of Unleavened Bread, when they sacrificed the Passover lamb, his disciples said to him, "Where do you want us to go and prepare for you to eat the Passover?" He sent two of his disciples and said to them, "Go into the city and a man will meet you, carrying a jar of water. Follow him. Wherever he enters, say to the master of the house, 'The Teacher says, "Where is my guest room where I may eat the Passover with my disciples?"' Then he will show you a large upper room furnished and ready. Make the preparations for us there." The disciples then went off, entered the city, and found it as he had told them; and they prepared the Passover.

When it was evening, he came with the Twelve. And as they reclined at table and were eating, Jesus said, "Amen, I say to you, one of you will betray me, one who is eating with me." They began to be distressed and to say to him, one by one, "Surely it is not I?" He said to them, "One of the Twelve, the one who dips with me into the dish. For the Son of Man indeed goes, as it is written of him, but woe to that man by whom the Son of Man is betrayed. It would be better for that man if he had never been born."

While they were eating, he took bread, said the blessing, broke it, and gave it to them, and said, "Take it; this is my body." Then he took a cup, gave thanks, and gave it to them, and they all drank from it. He said to them, "This is my blood of the covenant, which will be shed for many. Amen, I say to you, I shall not drink again the fruit of the vine until the day when I drink it new in the kingdom of God."

Action! Imagine choosing to have Thanksgiving Dinner with your new church friends instead of gathering with your family. By celebrating this most holy night together, Jesus' disciples are already saying that he is the most important person in their lives. Yet one of them is a traitor who has decided thirty pieces of silver are worth more than Jesus. This awkward revelation clearly mars the meal, but it also prepares us to realize that Jesus is preparing himself to be the sacrifice, the one perfect lamb.

Acknowledge: Read the passage a second time. Picture yourself among Jesus' disciples at table. What is in Jesus' heart as he gathers with his closest friends? He alone knows that this will be the Last Supper. What thoughts, feelings, or desires are you experiencing?

Relate: Lean over and talk to Jesus. Don't worry about the others; it's just the two of you now. What do you want to say to him?

Receive: Read the passage a third time. What does Jesus want to say to you?

Respond: Jesus deeply desires to be in communion with you. Enter into communion with him. Savor your deep friendship for a few minutes before moving on.

SUGGESTIONS FOR JOURNALING

1. How does Jesus' Last Supper look different in light of the passages we have read this week?
2. What part of today's prayer time was most meaningful to me?
3. Jesus wanted me to know that …
4. What does the word *sacrifice* mean to me?
5. How do I personally understand "communion"?
6. Next time I am at Mass, I will remember …

After you've journaled, close with a brief conversation thanking God for the gift you have experienced today. Let gratitude rise in your heart. Pray an Our Father.

+

The U.S. Bishops' "9 Days for Life" novena begins tomorrow. Learn more at www.9daysforlife.org

January 19 — Friday

Friday of the Second Week in Ordinary Time

Preparation: *Come, Holy Spirit, enlighten the eyes of my heart.* Be present to the God who is always present to you. Call to mind his loving care for you and spend the first minute of your prayer resting in the free, unearned gift of loving and being loved. Let gratitude rise in your heart.

***Lectio*:** We now turn to the final book in the Bible. The number 144,000 is a symbolically perfect number (twelve times twelve times a thousand). These souls were marked with God's seal in Revelation 7. God's grace has kept them safe through great trials, and he has not lost a single one of them. They inspire a great multitude to follow after them. How has the Lamb of God inspired them? Read the passage slowly and prayerfully.

REVELATION 14:1–5

Then I looked and there was the Lamb standing on Mount Zion, and with him a hundred and forty-four thousand who had his name and his Father's name written on their foreheads. I heard a sound from heaven like the sound of rushing water or a loud peal of thunder. The sound I heard was like that of harpists playing their harps. They were singing [what seemed to be] a new hymn before the throne, before the four living creatures and the elders. No one could learn this hymn except the hundred and forty-four thousand who had been ransomed from the earth. These are they who were not defiled with women; they are virgins and these are the ones who follow the Lamb wherever he goes. They have been ransomed as the firstfruits of the human race for God and the Lamb. On their lips no deceit has been found; they are unblemished.

***Meditatio*:** Is there a particular word, phrase, or idea that spoke to you?

What does it stir in your heart?

If you are to be like the Lamb of God, you will find yourself sharing in the rejection and passion of the Suffering Servant we prayed with yesterday. How do you feel about that? Read today's passage again.

***Oratio*:** Begin a conversation with God. Speak to him what is on your heart — your thoughts, feelings, fears, and desires.

***Contemplatio*:** Read the passage a third time. Now just receive what is on God's heart — his thoughts, feelings, and desires. Be not afraid! Spend some time receiving God's love and resting in it.

SUGGESTIONS FOR JOURNALING

1. I was not expecting …
2. The passage that most spoke to me was …
3. My greatest fear seems to be …
4. God wanted me to know …
5. I ended prayer wanting …

After you've journaled, close with thanksgiving to God for your prayer experience. Then pray an Our Father.

January 20 — Saturday

Saturday of the Second Week in Ordinary Time

REVIEW

In addition to the review below, or in place of it, you could choose to repeat any one of the meditations from the past week, if you find that to be a fruitful exercise.

Preparation: *Come, Holy Spirit, enlighten the eyes of my heart.* Call to mind God's loving care for you and spend the first minute of your prayer resting in the free, unearned gift of loving and being loved. Let gratitude rise in your heart.

Grace for the Day: What is the desire of your heart? Try to notice what you most deeply desire. Then share it with God in your own words, being confident that he loves you and wants to give you every blessing.

Week in Review: Flip back through your past week's journal entries. As you do, notice what emerged in the conversation. Here are some questions to help you:

1. Where did I notice God, and what was he doing or saying?
2. How did I respond to what God was doing?
3. I felt God's love most strongly when …
4. I found myself struggling with …
5. I'm grateful for …
6. This past week, my strongest sense, image, moment, or experience of God's loving presence was …
7. Now, the Lamb of God means …

Conclude by conversing with God about your week. Acknowledge what you have been experiencing. Relate it to him. Receive what he wants to give you. Respond to him. Then savor that image of God's loving presence and rest there for a minute or two. Close with an Our Father.

Week Eight

Discernment of Spirits

"How do I know it's really God that is speaking to me?" St. Ignatius of Loyola was a master at the discernment of spirits. He distinguishes between the spirit of God and the enemy. He says that if we are generally living for ourselves and engaging in mortal sin, the enemy spirit will try and keep us lulled into a false sense of security and comfort. For example, "Just a quick look at porn never hurt anyone." Or, "You can quit drinking tomorrow. Tonight, enjoy yourself." For this kind of person, the work of the Good Spirit will feel like a slap in the face or an alarm clock (some people use the phrase "spiritual 2x4") because the Good Spirit has to shake us out of our stupor so that we can see the danger to our soul.

On the other hand, for a person who is generally growing in faith, living for God, and trying to avoid sin, the work of the two spirits is the opposite. The enemy wants us to stop growing, so he will propose imaginary obstacles, discouragements, distractions, and confusion. Sometimes the enemy will try to convince you that you aren't holy enough and you need to do so much more for God. The voice of the enemy will be accusatory: "You're not good enough"; "You're broken"; "No one could love someone like you"; "You're doing it wrong; everyone else is having a better retreat than you"; "You missed a few days, you might as well quit, you could try again next year." These thoughts come with feelings of unrest, fear, sometimes panic. The Good Spirit, on the other hand, will be encouraging, supportive, and come with a sense of peace. The Good Spirit will remind us that we are loved, valued, and forgiven. Even when we need a "wake-up call," it will feel more like a gentle nudge.

Ignatius warned that spiritual people tend to go through patterns of consolation and desolation. Consolation is when we can feel God's love and have sense of peace and his presence; the right choices are obvious. Desolation is when we can't feel God's love and instead we hear the voice of the enemy more strongly; right seems wrong, and bad choices come easily. Think of consolation like a sunny day and desolation like a dark and stormy night. In desolation, we should not make a change, but keep walking on the road that we saw clearly when we were in consolation. In consolation, we should draw strength from God's love and prepare ourselves for when desolation comes again.

This pattern of easy and difficult, comfort and struggle, is to be expected on pilgrimages. Some days we feel strong and comforted, and we make progress easily. Other days are windy, cold, exhausting, and we find we have to put our heads down and just focus on putting one blistered foot in front of the other. The difficult times test your mettle and force you to face your fears and burdens. The times of resistance are actually the times of the most spiritual growth. So do not be discouraged if you have faced resistance, difficulties praying each day, and lots of struggles from inside of you and from outside. Resistance is a sign that you are on the right road and that, by overcoming obstacles, spiritual progress is happening. The only way to have a "bad pilgrimage" is to quit. Just keep walking, however slowly it may be, and you will eventually reach your goal.

Grace of the Week: We continue our journey by looking at the theme of discipleship in Mark's Gospel. Ask God for the grace to follow Jesus more closely as a faithful disciple.

January 21 — Sunday

Third Sunday in Ordinary Time

Preparation: *Come, Holy Spirit, enlighten the eyes of my heart.* Be present to the God who is always present to you. Call to mind his loving care for you and spend the first minute of your prayer resting in the free, unearned gift of loving and being loved. Let gratitude rise in your heart.

Set the Scene: Ask God for the grace to repent and believe in the Gospel so you can follow Jesus more closely. We meditated with this passage on our pilgrimage already, but now we have a chance to dive into it more deeply.

Let us return to the shores of Galilee. Picture the sea and the fishermen. Use your imagination to set the scene as you read the passage slowly and prayerfully.

MARK 1:14–20 (LECTIONARY)

After John had been arrested, Jesus came to Galilee proclaiming the gospel of God: "This is the time of fulfillment. The kingdom of God is at hand. Repent, and believe in the gospel."

As he passed by the Sea of Galilee, he saw Simon and his brother Andrew casting their nets into the sea; they were fishermen. Jesus said to them, "Come after me, and I will make you fishers of men." Then they abandoned their nets and followed him. He walked along a little farther and saw James, the son of Zebedee, and his brother John. They too were in a boat mending their nets. Then he called them. So they left their father Zebedee in the boat along with the hired men and followed him.

Action! Play the scene forward with your imagination. God created the world out of nothing and made human beings to be in union with him.

Through the envy of the Devil, sin entered the world and divided us from God and from one another. But God prepared a Savior for us, the Word-made-Flesh, who sacrificed himself for our sin. Now he reaches out and invites us into a relationship with him: to follow him, to remain with him.

Acknowledge: Read the passage a second time. The fishermen believe; they follow. What thoughts, feelings, and desires arise in your heart?

Relate: Can you leave everything to follow Jesus? Why or why not? Talk to Jesus about the call. What is he really asking of you? Why is he asking this? Picture yourself on the seashore with Jesus. Talk to him about everything.

Receive: Read the passage a third time. What does Jesus want to say to you? What does he want to give you? Can you open your heart to the gift of his friendship? We cannot fulfill the mission on our own, but Jesus will help you say "yes" to God's call and will give you whatever you need to accomplish the call.

Respond: Respond in whatever way you are able at this time. Know that the call of God is not fundamentally to go somewhere and do something, but rather to be with Jesus. Spend a few minutes with Jesus before moving on to the questions.

SUGGESTIONS FOR JOURNALING

1. God has been giving me …
2. God is inviting me to …
3. I feel …
4. My deepest desire is …
5. Jesus wanted me to know that …

After you've journaled, close with a brief conversation giving thanks to God for your prayer experience. Then pray an Our Father.

January 22 — Monday

Monday of the Third Week in Ordinary Time

DAY OF PRAYER FOR THE LEGAL PROTECTION OF UNBORN CHILDREN

In the United States of America, today is observed as a particular day of penance for violations against the dignity of the human person committed through acts of abortion. It is also a day of prayer for the full restoration of the legal guarantee to the right to life. Offer some fasting or another suitable penance today. Pray for a change of heart surrounding the dignity of human life.

Preparation: *Come, Holy Spirit, enlighten the eyes of my heart.* Be present to the God who is always present to you. Call to mind his loving care for you, and spend the first minute of your prayer resting in the free, unearned gift of loving and being loved. Let gratitude rise in your heart.

Set the Scene: Ask God for the grace to follow Jesus more closely as a faithful disciple.

Today we see the call of another disciple. Can you imagine Jesus entering your place of work and calling you to follow him? Tax collectors paid the occupying Romans a fixed sum for the right to collect taxes in their district. They could, however, levy whatever tax they wanted, collect however much they could get their hands on, and pocket the difference. This meant that tax collectors were often extorting more than the already heavy taxes and making themselves rich in the process. They were seen as traitors, sell-outs to a corrupt system where they and the Romans benefited from the powerlessness of the Jewish people. Picture the animosity between the tax collectors and the Jewish leaders. Even some of the other disciples probably questioned Jesus' call here. Read the passage and picture the scene in your mind.

MARK 2:13–17

Once again he went out along the sea. All the crowd came to him and he taught them. As he passed by, he saw Levi, son of Alphaeus, sitting at the customs post. He said to him, "Follow me." And he got up and followed him.

While he was at table in his house, many tax collectors and sinners sat with Jesus and his disciples; for there were many who followed him. Some scribes who were Pharisees saw that he was eating with sinners and tax collectors and said to his disciples, "Why does he eat with tax collectors and sinners?"

Jesus heard this and said to them [that], "Those who are well do not need a physician, but the sick do. I did not come to call the righteous but sinners."

Action! Jesus appears to be preaching repentance and then associating himself with the filthy rich, the worst members of society. The Pharisees, known for their faithfulness to the law, smell a hypocrite. Jesus sees it differently: He came to call sinners, and here they all are. How do you see it? Picture the party in your imagination. How is Jesus behaving? What kinds of conversations is he having? What is happening around him?

Acknowledge: Read the passage a second time. This time notice what is going on inside of you: your thoughts, feelings, and desires.

Relate: Don't be ashamed of your feelings, which are neither good nor bad. Simply notice what you are feeling and let it rise to the surface. Jesus is sitting on a bench outside the party. Sit with him and share your thoughts and feelings with him.

Receive: How does Jesus respond to what you have shared? What is in his heart for you? What does he want to say to you or give you? Don't think too hard, just notice what comes up. Read the passage a third time.

Respond: Can you catch a glimpse of Jesus' love for even the most hardened sinners, and his gentle, patient, persistent invitation? Do you feel the warmth of his love for you? Whatever you have received, respond to it with gratitude if you can. Then spend a couple minutes being with God who loves you and savors your friendship.

SUGGESTIONS FOR JOURNALING

1. What did Jesus see in Levi?
2. What did Jesus see in me when he called me?
3. Jesus wanted me to know that …
4. Who are the sinners that Jesus welcomes and eats with today?
5. Who am I being called to love and eat with, with Jesus' help?

After you've journaled, close by giving thanks to God for your prayer time today and then end with one Our Father.

January 23 — Tuesday

Tuesday of the Third Week in Ordinary Time

Preparation: *Come, Holy Spirit, enlighten the eyes of my heart.* Be present to the God who is always present to you. Call to mind his loving care for you and spend the first minute of your prayer resting in the free, unearned gift of loving and being loved. Let gratitude rise in your heart.

Set the Scene: Ask God for the grace to follow Jesus more closely as a faithful disciple.

You have been called by Jesus to follow him. You have heard him preach the Gospel and you have watched him cure the sick and cast out demons. Now it is your turn. You have been paired up with another disciple and off you go with no extra supplies, just your sandals and a walking stick. Read the passage slowly and picture the scene in your mind.

MARK 6:6B–13

He went around to the villages in the vicinity teaching. He summoned the Twelve and began to send them out two by two and gave them authority over unclean spirits. He instructed them to take nothing for the journey but a walking stick — no food, no sack, no money in their belts. They were, however, to wear sandals but not a second tunic.

He said to them, "Wherever you enter a house, stay there until you leave from there. Whatever place does not welcome you or listen to you, leave there and shake the dust off your feet in testimony against them."

So they went off and preached repentance. They drove out many demons, and they anointed with oil many who were sick and cured them.

Action! Imagine yourself and your companion going from village to village anointing the sick with oil, casting out demons, and announcing the kingdom of God. How do the people respond to you? Do you experience welcome, opposition, or indifference?

Acknowledge: Read the passage a second time. Notice what is going on inside of you: your thoughts, feelings, and desires. Are there any fears you are experiencing?

Relate: Let's talk to Jesus. Share with him how the mission is going. Most importantly, tell him how being sent on mission makes you feel.

Receive: How does Jesus respond to what you have shared? What is in his heart for you? What does he want to say to you or give you? Read the passage a third time.

Respond: Receive what Jesus wants to give you or what he wants to say to you. Respond to it, even if you feel the need to argue or complain. Then spend a couple minutes being with God who loves you and cherishes your "yes" to his call.

SUGGESTIONS FOR JOURNALING

1. Where did Jesus send me?
2. What was it like to be out on mission?
3. I found myself wishing that …
4. Jesus was trying to teach me …
5. What does it mean to see my home, place of work, or neighborhood as a mission field?

After you've journaled, close by giving thanks to God for trusting you with his mission and pray an Our Father.

January 24 — Wednesday

Wednesday of the Third Week in Ordinary Time

Preparation: *Come, Holy Spirit, enlighten the eyes of my heart.* Be present to the God who is always present to you. Call to mind his loving care for you and spend the first minute of your prayer resting in the free, unearned gift of loving and being loved. Let gratitude rise in your heart.

Set the Scene: Ask God for the grace to follow Jesus more closely as a faithful disciple.

Our passage today has four separate scenes. First, Jesus asks his disciples an important question, and Peter volunteers the right answer. Then, Jesus begins to teach his disciples that, contrary to popular opinion, the Messiah will be a suffering servant rather than a conquering king. Peter takes Jesus off to the side to correct him, but finds himself the subject of correction. Finally, Jesus' public preaching begins to reflect the content of these private conversations. Follow the conversation from the perspective of the disciples.

MARK 8:27–38

Now Jesus and his disciples set out for the villages of Caesarea Philippi. Along the way he asked his disciples, "Who do people say that I am?" They said in reply, "John the Baptist, others Elijah, still others one of the prophets." And he asked them, "But who do you say that I am?" Peter said to him in reply, "You are the Messiah." Then he warned them not to tell anyone about him.

He began to teach them that the Son of Man must suffer greatly and be rejected by the elders, the chief priests, and the scribes, and be killed, and rise after three days. He spoke this openly. Then Peter took him aside and began to rebuke him. At this he turned around and, looking at his disciples, rebuked Peter and said, "Get be-

hind me, Satan. You are thinking not as God does, but as human beings do."

He summoned the crowd with his disciples and said to them, "Whoever wishes to come after me must deny himself, take up his cross, and follow me. For whoever wishes to save his life will lose it, but whoever loses his life for my sake and that of the gospel will save it. What profit is there for one to gain the whole world and forfeit his life? What could one give in exchange for his life? Whoever is ashamed of me and of my words in this faithless and sinful generation, the Son of Man will be ashamed of when he comes in his Father's glory with the holy angels."

Action! This scene appears halfway through the Gospel of Mark and marks a decisive turning point. Jesus is a wildly popular public figure. Popular opinion holds that Jesus is a prophet, perhaps even a reincarnation of the recently-beheaded John the Baptist. Jesus' closest disciples are convinced that he is the Anointed One, the new King of the Jews who will set all things right. They expect the Messiah to establish an earthly kingdom of prosperity and peace. But God's ways are not our ways. Would they have followed Jesus as eagerly if they had known what they were signing up for?

Acknowledge: Read the passage a second time. This time notice what is going on inside of you: your thoughts, feelings, and desires. Would you have followed Jesus if you knew what he was really calling you to? How did your expectations of your vocation or of discipleship differ from the reality you have experienced?

Relate: Take Jesus aside and speak to him. Ask him whatever questions are on your heart and be honest with him. There's no reason to be ashamed or to hide anything from him, even if you find yourself frustrated or confused.

Receive: How does Jesus respond to what you have shared? What is in his heart for you? What does he want to say to you or give you? Know that it comes from a place of his deep love for you. Read the passage a third time.

Respond: Jesus promises a glorious kingdom, one more amazing than the disciples could have ever imagined, but it will only appear at the end of a long and, at times, painful life of faithful service to the true king. The mission is difficult, but the rewards are out of this world. Respond to what Jesus gave you, then spend a couple minutes in prayerful contemplation of the king and his kingdom.

SUGGESTIONS FOR JOURNALING

1. What does the kingdom of God mean to me?
2. In what ways have I had to take up my cross as I followed Jesus?
3. How do I see the suffering and passion of Jesus as an act of love?
4. Jesus wanted to give me confidence that …
5. In what ways can I love more purely and sacrificially?

After you've journaled, close by giving thanks to God for your prayer time today and then end with an Our Father.

January 25 — Thursday

The Conversion of Saint Paul, Apostle

Why did Saul of Tarsus, zealous Jewish student of the law and persecutor of Christians, become Paul, an apostle who would die for the Jesus he had once blasphemed? Saul was present when Stephen was martyred and consented to the stoning (see Acts 7:58; 8:1). Perhaps Stephen loved his enemies and prayed for those who persecuted him. Jesus met Saul in a vision on the road to Damascus. He opened his eyes to the deeper meaning of the Scriptures he thought he knew so well. Saint Paul witnessed to Jesus for the rest of his life and joined Stephen in a martyr's death. By the prayers of Saint Paul, may your eyes be opened to God's word in today's Scripture passage.

Preparation: *Come, Holy Spirit, enlighten the eyes of my heart.* Be present to the God who is always present to you. Call to mind his loving care for you and spend the first minute of your prayer resting in the free, unearned gift of loving and being loved. Let gratitude rise in your heart.

Set the Scene: Ask God for the grace to follow Jesus more closely as a faithful disciple.

Our Scripture passage speaks of both the end of the Temple and the end of the world. The Jews saw the Temple as a sort of creation in miniature. It had decorations depicting the heavens and the earth. It featured an enormous cauldron of water called "the sea" (2 Chr 4:2–5). It was meant to gather all creation into the perfect worship of the Creator. To the Jews, the destruction of the Temple foreshadowed the end of the world. In today's passage, Jesus leaves the Temple and heads up the Mount of Olives, which has a good view of the whole city. The Temple would have dominated the skyline. Read the passage and picture the scene in your mind.

MARK 13:1–13

As he was making his way out of the temple area one of his disciples said to him, "Look, teacher, what stones and what buildings!" Jesus said to him, "Do you see these great buildings? There will not be one stone left upon another that will not be thrown down." As he was sitting on the Mount of Olives opposite the temple area, Peter, James, John, and Andrew asked him privately, "Tell us, when will this happen, and what sign will there be when all these things are about to come to an end?" Jesus began to say to them, "See that no one deceives you. Many will come in my name saying, 'I am he,' and they will deceive many. When you hear of wars and reports of wars do not be alarmed; such things must happen, but it will not yet be the end. Nation will rise against nation and kingdom against kingdom. There will be earthquakes from place to place and there will be famines. These are the beginnings of the labor pains.

"Watch out for yourselves. They will hand you over to the courts. You will be beaten in synagogues. You will be arraigned before governors and kings because of me, as a witness before them. But the gospel must first be preached to all nations. When they lead you away and hand you over, do not worry beforehand about what you are to say. But say whatever will be given to you at that hour. For it will not be you who are speaking but the holy Spirit. Brother will hand over brother to death, and the father his child; children will rise up against parents and have them put to death. You will be hated by all because of my name. But the one who perseveres to the end will be saved."

Action! As the conversation continues, Jesus shifts their attention from grand events to individual tribulations. He alone knows that he is going to face the same abuse he predicts for his disciples. No disciple is greater than his master; if the master has suffered, the disciples must, too. Jesus wants to make sure his followers do not lose heart. What does he want to make sure they do? What must they avoid?

Acknowledge: Read the passage a second time. This time notice what is going on inside of you: your thoughts, feelings, and desires. Are any fears rising to the surface?

Relate: Sit next to Jesus on the Mount of Olives. See the sorrow in his heart that the very people he loves and has come to save will reject him, just like Saul did. Share with Jesus what is on your heart.

Receive: How does Jesus respond to what you have shared? What is in his heart for you? What does he want to say to you or give you? Read the passage a third time.

Respond: Jesus will be faithful to the Father even unto death. He wants you to do the same. What will he give you? What does he say to you? How does he reassure you? Respond to whatever you have received and then be with him for a few minutes.

SUGGESTIONS FOR JOURNALING

1. The Temple was enormous. It looked like it would stand forever. Yet just forty years after Christ, the people of Palestine would revolt and the Romans would march upon the city, burn it down, and demolish the Temple completely. It has never been rebuilt. What are some things that look so solid but will soon be destroyed?
2. What are the things that I can depend on, that will remain solid no matter what?
3. When I think of the end of the world, I'm afraid that …
4. Jesus assures me that …
5. In today's prayer I realized …

After you've journaled, close by giving thanks to God for his unshakable love for you experienced in your prayer time today. Then pray an Our Father.

January 26 — Friday

Saints Timothy and Titus, Bishops

Saint Timothy was the son of a pagan father and a Hebrew-Christian mother, Eunice (see 2 Tm 1:5). He was a disciple of Saint Paul and accompanied him on his journeys. Paul consecrated him bishop of Ephesus. Saint Titus was also a friend and disciple of Paul, who ordained him bishop of Crete. Paul wrote three pastoral letters to these two disciples. It is fitting that the day after we celebrate Paul's conversion, we celebrate the feasts of two men whom Paul mentored in the Christian life.

Preparation: *Come, Holy Spirit, enlighten the eyes of my heart.* Be present to the God who is always present to you. Call to mind his loving care for you and spend the first minute of your prayer resting in the free, unearned gift of loving and being loved. Let gratitude rise in your heart.

Set the Scene: Ask God for the grace to follow Jesus more closely as a faithful disciple. Jesus predicted several times that he would suffer greatly, die on the cross, and then rise from the dead. His disciples were surprised when everything happened just as he had promised. How often have we been surprised when God answered prayer or when Church teaching has turned out to be true? Instead of judging the apostles, we should consider our own faith. Read the passage slowly and prayerfully, and use your imagination to make the scenes come alive.

MARK 16:9–20

When he had risen, early on the first day of the week, he appeared first to Mary Magdalene, out of whom he had driven seven demons. She went and told his companions who were mourning and weeping. When they heard that he was alive and had been seen by her, they did not believe. After this he appeared in another form to two of them walking along on their way to the country. They re-

turned and told the others; but they did not believe them either. [But] later, as the eleven were at table, he appeared to them and rebuked them for their unbelief and hardness of heart because they had not believed those who saw him after he had been raised. He said to them, "Go into the whole world and proclaim the gospel to every creature. Whoever believes and is baptized will be saved; whoever does not believe will be condemned. These signs will accompany those who believe: in my name they will drive out demons, they will speak new languages. They will pick up serpents [with their hands], and if they drink any deadly thing, it will not harm them. They will lay hands on the sick, and they will recover."

So then the Lord Jesus, after he spoke to them, was taken up into heaven and took his seat at the right hand of God. But they went forth and preached everywhere, while the Lord worked with them and confirmed the word through accompanying signs.

Action! Picture each scene, but especially the upper room at the moment when Jesus appears in the middle of the apostles' meal. What are they thinking and feeling? All but one of them would eventually be martyred for their faith in Jesus. Picture them preaching everywhere, casting out demons and speaking new languages. At some point in the recent or distant past, your own ancestors met a Timothy, Titus, or one of their successors and came to believe in Jesus for themselves. What does this passage say to you?

Acknowledge: Read the passage a second time. This time notice what is going on inside of you: your thoughts, feelings, and desires.

Relate: You can't see Jesus seated at the right hand of God, but he can clearly see you and hear you. Speak to him in your heart. Share your thoughts, feelings, and desires with him.

Receive: How does Jesus respond to what you have shared? What does he want to say to you or give you? What is in his heart for you? Read the passage a third time.

Respond: Whatever Jesus gives you, respond to it. Then spend a couple minutes being with God who always gazes at you with love.

SUGGESTIONS FOR JOURNALING

1. In what ways have I struggled to believe in the Gospel message?
2. Are there people who have a hard time believing me when I share the Good News with them? How does Jesus want to help me?
3. I have seen the power of Jesus working through his disciples when …
4. I feel called to …
5. Who needs to hear the Good News? Spend a few minutes praying for that person or persons.

After you've journaled, close by giving thanks to God for his power and his presence in your prayer time today. Then close with an Our Father.

January 27 — Saturday

Saturday of the Third Week in Ordinary Time

REVIEW

In addition to the review below, or in place of it, you could choose to repeat any one of the meditations from the past week, if you find that to be a fruitful exercise.

Preparation: *Come, Holy Spirit, enlighten the eyes of my heart.* Call to mind God's loving care for you and spend the first minute of your prayer resting in the free, unearned gift of loving and being loved. Let gratitude rise in your heart.

Grace for the Day: What is the desire of your heart? Try to notice what you most deeply desire. Then share it with God in your own words, being confident that he loves you and wants to give you every blessing.

Week in Review: Flip back through your past week's journal entries. As you do, notice what emerged in the conversation. Here are some questions to help you:

1. Where did I notice God, and what was he doing or saying?
2. How did I respond to what God was doing?
3. I felt God's love most strongly when …
4. I found myself struggling with …
5. I'm grateful for …
6. This past week, my strongest sense, image, moment, or experience of God's loving presence was …

Conclude by conversing with God about your week. Acknowledge what you have been experiencing. Relate it to him. Receive what he wants to give you. Respond to him. Then savor that image of God's loving presence and rest there for a minute or two. Close with an Our Father.

Week Nine

The Feast of the Presentation

Saint Luke is the only Gospel writer who records the presentation of Jesus in the Temple (see Lk 2:22–40). Jewish law required the purification of a mother forty days after the birth of a male child (Lv 12:1–8). It also stipulated that the firstborn belonged to the priests. A firstborn cow, sheep, or goat would be sacrificed to God by the priest. But a firstborn child would be "bought back" by a payment of money (Ex 13:11–16, Nm 18:15–16).

The way Saint Luke writes about Jesus' presentation, Mary and Joseph are not "buying back" (redeeming) their Son, but presenting him. The unseen God has been worshiped in this Temple for centuries. Now God himself, in the person of Jesus in the form of a humble babe, is visiting his own Temple. His visit does not go without notice. Simeon and Anna symbolize the whole Old Testament, grown old waiting for God's promises to be fulfilled. And they are not disappointed.

Remember back at the beginning of Advent, how we were told to watch? These two old people are the only ones still watching. Though their earthly eyes may be dimmed by old age, God has enlightened the eyes of their hearts. They can see the One that all have been waiting for but no one else recognizes. They perfectly symbolize what our *Oriens* pilgrimage has been all about.

Grace of the Week: We continue our journey by drawing from Scripture passages that touch on the themes of light and darkness. At your baptism you received the Light of Christ. Pray that the light of faith in Christ, given to you at your baptism, may burn ever brighter.

January 28 — Sunday

The Fourth Sunday in Ordinary Time

Preparation: *Come, Holy Spirit, enlighten the eyes of my heart.* Call to mind God's loving care for you and spend the first minute of your prayer resting in the free, unearned gift of loving and being loved. Let gratitude rise in your heart.

***Lectio*:** Ask God that the light of faith in Christ, given to you at your baptism, may burn ever brighter.

This passage appears at the very end of Moses' life. God met him at the burning bush and called him to free the Israelites from slavery in Egypt. After forty years of wandering, they are about to enter the Promised Land. Moses is 120 years old, and he will only be able to gaze on the land from afar. He is comforted by the fact that God will continue to lead the people. Read the passage slowly and prayerfully.

DEUTERONOMY 18:15–20 (LECTIONARY)

Moses spoke to all the people, saying: "A prophet like me will the LORD, your God, raise up for you from among your own kin; to him you shall listen. This is exactly what you requested of the LORD, your God, at Horeb on the day of the assembly, when you said, 'Let us not again hear the voice of the LORD, our God, nor see this great fire any more, lest we die.' And the LORD said to me, 'This was well said. I will raise up for them a prophet like you from among their kin, and will put my words into his mouth; he shall tell them all that I command him. Whoever will not listen to my words which he speaks in my name, I myself will make him answer for it. But if a prophet presumes to speak in my name an oracle that I have not commanded him to speak, or speaks in the name of other gods, he shall die.'"

***Meditatio*:** There will be many prophets. Some will speak falsely or will speak in the name of false gods. Some discernment will be needed. But one day there will be a new Moses, a prophet who will free the people from slavery to sin and death. Are we careful about the voices we listen to? Do we know the Good Shepherd and follow his voice?

Read the passage a second time.

***Oratio*:** Have you ever felt lost in the desert? Have you struggled to hear God's voice or to understand what he wanted to say to you? Tell him about it. Speak to the burning bush yourself and share your thoughts, fears, and desires with the God who loves you.

***Contemplatio*:** Read the passage a third time. This time just receive what God wants to give you or say to you. He loves you as much as he loves Moses. Receive what is in God's heart for you and rest in his loving care for a few minutes.

SUGGESTIONS FOR JOURNALING

1. How is Jesus a prophet like Moses?
2. What can Moses teach me about my own "yes" to God's call?
3. My strongest thought, feeling, or desire was …
4. God wanted me to know …
5. I feel called to …

Spend a minute thanking God for your prayer time today and for the gift of nine weeks of *Oriens*. Close with the Our Father.

January 29 — Monday

Monday of the Fourth Week in Ordinary Time

Preparation: *Come, Holy Spirit, enlighten the eyes of my heart.* Be present to the God who is always present to you. Call to mind his loving care for you and spend the first minute of your prayer resting in the free, unearned gift of loving and being loved. Let gratitude rise in your heart.

***Lectio*:** Ask God that the light of faith in Christ, given to you at your baptism, may burn ever brighter.

During the Christmas season we read all the nativity stories except one. Saint John has a different perspective on the origins of the Messiah. Read the passage slowly and try to understand the symbolism.

JOHN 1:1–9

In the beginning was the Word,
and the Word was with God,
and the Word was God.
He was in the beginning with God.
All things came to be through him,
and without him nothing came to be.
What came to be through him was life,
and this life was the light of the human race;
the light shines in the darkness,
and the darkness has not overcome it.

A man named John was sent from God. He came for testimony, to testify to the light, so that all might believe through him. He was not the light, but came to testify to the light. The true light, which enlightens everyone, was coming into the world.

***Meditatio*:** God's word is intimately connected with him, yet distinct from him. He is life, and he is light. It is obvious, then, from the very beginning that the enemies of the Word are death and darkness. Light also serves to reveal, to "enlighten." Turn over these ideas in your mind, then read the passage again.

***Oratio*:** You yourself have believed in the Word and have come to know him and love him. Speak your own words to the Word.

***Contemplatio*:** Read the passage a third time. All things were made through him, and that includes you. Enter into a communion of mind and heart with the Word. Then rest in God's abiding presence for a little while.

SUGGESTIONS FOR JOURNALING

1. How has God's light been shining in my darkness?
1. I was enlightened by …
2. I experience God's life when …
3. How am I called to bear witness to the light?

After you've journaled, close with a brief conversation with God giving thanks for your prayer experience. Then pray an Our Father.

January 30 — Tuesday

Tuesday of the Fourth Week in Ordinary Time

Preparation: *Come, Holy Spirit, enlighten the eyes of my heart.* Be present to the God who is always present to you. Call to mind his loving care for you and spend the first minute of your prayer resting in the free, unearned gift of loving and being loved. Let gratitude rise in your heart.

***Lectio*:** Ask God that the light of faith in Christ, given to you at your baptism, may burn ever brighter.

The word of God has been rejected by many. But to those who accept him, he shares his own status as Son of God. He himself is the fullness of God and the glory of God. Read the passage slowly.

JOHN 1:9–18

The true light, which enlightens everyone, was coming into the world.

He was in the world,
and the world came to be through him,
but the world did not know him.
He came to what was his own,
but his own people did not accept him.

But to those who did accept him he gave power to become children of God, to those who believe in his name, who were born not by natural generation nor by human choice nor by a man's decision but of God.

And the Word became flesh
and made his dwelling among us,
and we saw his glory,

the glory as of the Father's only Son,
full of grace and truth.

John testified to him and cried out, saying, "This was he of whom I said, 'The one who is coming after me ranks ahead of me because he existed before me.'" From his fullness we have all received, grace in place of grace, because while the law was given through Moses, grace and truth came through Jesus Christ. No one has ever seen God. The only Son, God, who is at the Father's side, has revealed him.

***Meditatio*:** The ancients compared meditating to a cow chewing its cud. Turn over these words in your mind. How have I faced rejection for following God? How do I feel as a child of God? How have I beheld the Father's glory in his Son? After turning over these ideas in your mind, read the passage again.

***Oratio*:** Open your heart to the word of God. Share what is in your heart and receive what is in his heart.

***Contemplatio*:** Read the passage a third time. Jesus lives, as it were, in his Father's heart. And he wants us there with him. Spend a little while abiding in God and letting God abide in you.

SUGGESTIONS FOR JOURNALING

1. When have I experienced being a child of God?
2. When have I rejected God's word, God's light, God's life?
3. I beheld the glory of God when …
4. The time I felt closest to God was …
5. I feel God calling me to …

After you've journaled, close with a brief conversation with God giving thanks for your prayer experience. Then pray an Our Father.

January 31 — Wednesday

Wednesday of the Fourth Week in Ordinary Time

Preparation: *Come, Holy Spirit, enlighten the eyes of my heart.* Be present to the God who is always present to you. Call to mind his loving care for you and spend the first minute of your prayer resting in the free, unearned gift of loving and being loved. Let gratitude rise in your heart.

***Lectio*:** Ask God that the light of faith in Christ, given to you at your baptism, may burn ever brighter.

The light of Christ shows us what true love looks like and what it means to be a child of God. The people around us often seem to be sleep walking in the darkness, bumping into things and hurting themselves and others. But we must be different; we are called to live in the light as God's beloved children. Read the passage slowly and prayerfully.

EPHESIANS 5:1–14

So be imitators of God, as beloved children, and live in love, as Christ loved us and handed himself over for us as a sacrificial offering to God for a fragrant aroma. Immorality or any impurity or greed must not even be mentioned among you, as is fitting among holy ones, no obscenity or silly or suggestive talk, which is out of place, but instead, thanksgiving. Be sure of this, that no immoral or impure or greedy person, that is, an idolater, has any inheritance in the kingdom of Christ and of God.

Let no one deceive you with empty arguments, for because of these things the wrath of God is coming upon the disobedient. So do not be associated with them. For you were once darkness, but now you are light in the Lord. Live as children of light, for light produces every kind of goodness and righteousness and truth. Try to learn what is pleasing to the Lord. Take no part in the fruitless works

> *of darkness; rather expose them, for it is shameful even to mention the things done by them in secret; but everything exposed by the light becomes visible, for everything that becomes visible is light. Therefore, it says:*
>
> > *"Awake, O sleeper,*
> > *and arise from the dead,*
> > *and Christ will give you light."*

***Meditatio*:** How is Christ's light shining more brightly now than when you first began your Advent and Christmas pilgrimage? Do you feel you have "awakened" to a new way of thinking, praying, or living? Read the passage again.

***Oratio*:** Talk to God about what is in your heart. Start with thanksgiving for the ways he has enlightened you. How do you feel God calling you to be more a child of the light? Ask him for the help you need to share his love by your words and actions.

***Contemplatio*:** Read the passage a third time. Receive what is in God's heart for you — his thoughts and feelings and desires. Receive whatever he wants to give you, then rest in the light of his love.

SUGGESTIONS FOR JOURNALING

1. I notice the darkness of the world most strongly when …
2. I feel most awake and alive when …
3. These few weeks have helped me to …
4. I ended prayer wanting …
5. I sense the Lord calling me to a new way of acting, thinking, or living by …

After you've journaled, close by giving thanks to God for your prayer time today and then end with the Our Father.

February 1 — Thursday

Thursday of the Fourth Week in Ordinary Time

Preparation: *Come, Holy Spirit, enlighten the eyes of my heart.* Be present to the God who is always present to you. Call to mind his loving care for you and spend the first minute of your prayer resting in the free, unearned gift of loving and being loved. Let gratitude rise in your heart.

***Lectio*:** In the end, love wins. God conquers the enemy, good defeats evil, and the light conquers the darkness forever and ever. God's servants shall worship him, and they shall see his face. Notice what word or phrase strikes you as you read this passage slowly and prayerfully.

REVELATION 21:9–12, 22–27; 22:1–5

One of the seven angels who held the seven bowls filled with the seven last plagues came and said to me, "Come here. I will show you the bride, the wife of the Lamb." He took me in spirit to a great, high mountain and showed me the holy city Jerusalem coming down out of heaven from God. It gleamed with the splendor of God. Its radiance was like that of a precious stone, like jasper, clear as crystal. It had a massive, high wall, with twelve gates where twelve angels were stationed and on which names were inscribed, [the names] of the twelve tribes of the Israelites.

I saw no temple in the city, for its temple is the Lord God almighty and the Lamb. The city had no need of sun or moon to shine on it, for the glory of God gave it light, and its lamp was the Lamb. The nations will walk by its light, and to it the kings of the earth will bring their treasure. During the day its gates will never be shut, and there will be no night there. The treasure and wealth of the nations will be brought there, but nothing unclean will enter it, nor any[one] who does abominable things or tells lies. Only those will enter whose names are written in the Lamb's book of life.

Then the angel showed me the river of life-giving water, sparkling like crystal, flowing from the throne of God and of the Lamb down the middle of its street. On either side of the river grew the tree of life that produces fruit twelve times a year, once each month; the leaves of the trees serve as medicine for the nations. Nothing accursed will be found there anymore. The throne of God and of the Lamb will be in it, and his servants will worship him. They will look upon his face, and his name will be on their foreheads. Night will be no more, nor will they need light from lamp or sun, for the Lord God shall give them light, and they shall reign forever and ever.

***Meditatio*:** This life is full of light and darkness. But our hearts should be full of light as we press on to the kingdom of light. What thoughts, feelings, and desires are rising in your heart as you read these words? Read the passage again. Notice the part that most speaks to you.

***Oratio*:** Bring your thoughts, feelings, and desires to God. Speak to him from your heart.

***Contemplatio*:** Read the passage a third time, or just the part that speaks to you. Receive what is in God's heart for you. We will never experience the fullness of communion here on earth, but we will experience enough to glimpse what is waiting for us. Gaze on the Father and let him gaze upon you with love.

SUGGESTIONS FOR JOURNALING

1. Sometimes I struggle to believe that …
2. My heart breaks when …
3. I most deeply desire …
4. God has even more to give. I ended prayer yearning for …
5. I most look forward to a heaven where …

After you've journaled, close by giving thanks to God for your prayer time today. Then close with an Our Father.

February 2 — Friday

Feast of the Presentation of the Lord

"The *presentation of Jesus in the temple* shows him to be the firstborn Son who belongs to the Lord. With Simeon and Anna, all Israel awaits its *encounter* with the Savior — the name given to this event in the Byzantine tradition. Jesus is recognized as the long-expected Messiah, the 'light to the nations' and the 'glory of Israel,' but also 'a sign that is spoken against.' The sword of sorrow predicted for Mary announces Christ's perfect and unique oblation on the cross that will impart the salvation God had 'prepared in the presence of all peoples.'" (CCC 529)

Preparation: *Come, Holy Spirit, enlighten the eyes of my heart.* Be present to the God who is always present to you. Call to mind his loving care for you and spend the first minute of your prayer resting in the free, unearned gift of loving and being loved. Let gratitude rise in your heart.

Set the Scene: The Temple in Jerusalem is the largest and most impressive building most Jews had ever seen. But soon it will all be destroyed, replaced by the one perfect sacrifice and the New Covenant in the blood of Jesus. In this humble moment, God enters his Temple. Read the passage and picture the enormous Temple, the elderly couple, and the babe who is God from God and Light from Light.

LUKE 2:22–40 (LECTIONARY)

When the days were completed for their purification according to the law of Moses, Mary and Joseph took Jesus up to Jerusalem to present him to the Lord, just as it is written in the law of the Lord, Every male that opens the womb shall be consecrated to the Lord, *and to offer the sacrifice of* a pair of turtledoves or two young pigeons, *in accordance with the dictate in the law of the Lord. Now there was a man in Jerusalem whose name was Simeon.*

This man was righteous and devout, awaiting the consolation of Israel, and the Holy Spirit was upon him. It had been revealed to him by the Holy Spirit that he should not see death before he had seen the Christ of the Lord. He came in the Spirit into the temple; and when the parents brought in the child Jesus to perform the custom of the law in regard to him, he took him into his arms and blessed God, saying:

"Now, Master, you may let your servant go
in peace, according to your word,
for my eyes have seen your salvation,
which you prepared in sight of all the peoples:
a light for revelation to the Gentiles,
and glory for your people Israel."

The child's father and mother were amazed at what was said about him; and Simeon blessed them and said to Mary his mother, "Behold, this child is destined for the fall and rise of many in Israel, and to be a sign that will be contradicted — and you yourself a sword will pierce — so that the thoughts of many hearts may be revealed." There was also a prophetess, Anna, the daughter of Phanuel, of the tribe of Asher. She was advanced in years, having lived seven years with her husband after her marriage, and then as a widow until she was eighty-four. She never left the temple, but worshiped night and day with fasting and prayer. And coming forward at that very time, she gave thanks to God and spoke about the child to all who were awaiting the redemption of Jerusalem.

When they had fulfilled all the prescriptions of the law of the Lord, they returned to Galilee, to their own town of Nazareth. The child grew and became strong, filled with wisdom; and the favor of God was upon him.

Action! The rest of the people are going about their business, never realizing the amazing thing that is happening. Simeon and Anna see more because they see with the eyes of faith. Notice what is going on in their hearts. What does your faith enable you to see in this scene? Use your imagination.

Acknowledge: Read the passage a second time. Notice what part speaks to you. What is going on inside of you? How does your heart leap for joy? What do you feel and experience? Ask Mary to let you hold her child.

Relate: Speak to the Christ Child, heart to heart. Invite him into your heart.

Receive: Read the passage a third time, but now just focus on the part that speaks to you. Open your heart to receive all that God wants to give you.

Respond: Jesus lives in the heart of every believer. Welcome him into your heart. Let your heart enter into a deeper communion with the Word-made-Flesh. Let him cast out your darkness and fill you with his pure light.

SUGGESTIONS FOR JOURNALING

1. I was surprised by …
2. The part that most spoke to me was …
3. The greatest gift God has given me on this pilgrimage is …
4. In exchange, I found God wanting me to give him …
5. I ended prayer wanting …

After you've journaled, close with a brief conversation and give thanks to God. Then pray an Our Father.

Once a Pilgrim, Always a Pilgrim

Pilgrimages always seem to end abruptly. You strive to reach your destination, you struggle on the road, you wonder if you'll ever get there. Then you realize it's the final day, the final miles, and the place of pilgrimage is just over the next hill! You have made it to your destination. You bask in the feeling of success, promise to stay in touch with your fellow pilgrims, and struggle to explain to your family what has happened to you.

Then it is back to your old life. But the old life looks different now; the journey has changed you. You see yourself, God, and the world around you in a different light. Hopefully you, too, have become a light.

Christmas time has lit your heart with the warmth and light of God's love. Keep tending your candle! Keep burning and glowing with the light of faith. Carry that light to the dark corners of the world so that the light of God's love will spread to every heart and home.

REVIEW OF REVIEWS

When you have a little time, flip back to the very first day of your pilgrimage, Sunday, December 3, and look at how it all began. Then take a journey through the eight Saturday review days. Notice what was coming up. Reflect on where you have been and how God has been with you on the journey. Notice how the journey has changed you.

SUGGESTIONS FOR JOURNALING

1. How did God meet me on the road?
2. There's so much! But the part that most spoke to me was …
3. God was telling me that …
4. I was able to let go of …
5. The deepest desire that has emerged in my heart was …
6. The greatest gift God has given me on this pilgrimage is …
7. In exchange, I found God asked me to give him the gift of …
8. I would describe my newfound relationship with God as …

Acknowledge what the pilgrimage meant to you. Relate it to God. Receive what he wants to give you. Respond to him. Then savor God's loving presence and rest there for a minute or two. Close with an Our Father.

The Journey Continues

I always tell pilgrims that they need to keep walking. Our journey is never done until we *come to the end of our pilgrimage and enter the presence of God*. Here are some suggestions for you to continue the journey:

- Buy a journal. At the end of each day, answer two questions: 1) Where did I see God today? 2) What was God doing? Use the ARRR prayer form (on page 305) to pray with your daily experiences and journal the fruits of your prayer.
- On the following pages, I give you outlines for four different forms of prayer. You might even want to tear out those pages and keep them with your journal.
- Start praying with the daily Scripture readings. You can find each day's readings at usccb.org/bible/readings/. Depending on the reading, you can use *Lectio Divina* or Imaginative Prayer for your prayer each day (see the Prayer Outlines on pages 301 and 303) .
- Subscribe to a monthly missal. I have used *Magnificat* for years, and I find it very helpful. It includes prayer for morning and evening, the daily readings, and some reflections and additional prayers. There are many other monthly missals to choose from, and all of them will help you pray daily.
- Need more help journaling? Check out the *Monk Manual* at monkmanual.com. This resource provides reflection space and prompts for you on a daily, weekly, and monthly basis. It helps you live with more reflection and purpose.
- Another great journal option is *Every Sacred Sunday*, which has readings and journal space for Sundays and holy days. Check it out at everysacredsunday.com.
- Subscribe to my homily podcast at pilgrimpriest.us/podcast.
- OSV has a number of Bible study resources. Browse their offerings at www.osvcatholicbookstore.com/product-category/bibles-bible-studies. Consider not only participating in a Bible study, but actually leading one at your local church or in

your home.

- Lent is coming up soon. Start reflecting and praying about a theme for Lent and how to live Lent more intentionally.
- Consider making a real, honest-to-goodness walking pilgrimage. My diocese hosts the Walk to Mary every year, a one-day walking pilgrimage. Learn more at walktomary.com. Check out my website, pilgrimpriest.us, for the article "A Step-by-Step Guide to Walking Pilgrimages."

Prayer Outlines

Lectio Divina

Lectio divina can be used with any passage from Scripture. The key is to use Scripture as a conversation starter for a deep, personal conversation with the God who inspired it. Don't rush each step; let them naturally unfold. Remember that the goal is spending quality time with the God who loves you. As you Read, Think, Talk, and Listen, you will learn to spend time with God like an old friend.

Preparation: *Come, Holy Spirit, enlighten the eyes of my heart.* Be present to the God who is always present to you. Call to mind his loving care for you and spend the first minute of your prayer resting in the free, unearned gift of loving and being loved. Let gratitude rise in your heart.

***Lectio*:** Ask God for whatever grace it is you desire to receive in today's prayer time. Read the passage through, slowly and prayerfully.

***Meditatio*:** Read the passage again. Turn it over in your mind. The ancients compared meditation to a cow chewing its cud. What was the cultural context? What did the author mean? Perhaps a particular word, phrase, or idea speaks to you. Perhaps it connects to a previous meditation or another Scripture passage. What are your feelings as you read the passage?

***Oratio*:** Prayer must be a conversation between persons. Turn to God and begin a conversation with him. Speak to him what is on your heart — your thoughts, feelings, fears, and desires.

***Contemplatio*:** Read the passage a third time. Now just receive what is on God's heart — his thoughts, feelings, and desires. Spend some time receiving God's love and resting in it. Prayer is experiencing how our Father looks at us with love. Holiness is learning to live in his loving gaze every moment of our life.

SUGGESTIONS FOR JOURNALING

Journaling isn't an essential part of the prayer, but I find it helps me to deepen the experience when I put into words what was happening in the prayer time. You might find questions like these helpful, or you might make your own list of journal questions:

1. The part that most spoke to me was …
2. What I brought to the Lord was …
3. God gave me …
4. I received a new insight, understanding, or sense of myself when s…
5. Apply something from the passage to your own life. (For example, a passage about John the Baptist: Who pointed out Jesus to me? When did I point out Jesus to another person, or what virtue of John the Baptist do I feel called to imitate?)

After you've journaled, close with a brief conversation giving thanks to God for the prayer time together. End with an Our Father or another favorite prayer.

Imaginative Prayer

Imaginative prayer helps us disconnect from the circumstances of our present moment in order to connect us with the deep reality of God's loving, invisible presence with us right now. The goal is not to build great imaginary castles in the air but to look into the Bible and through it encounter the God who was present in the moment when the biblical passage was written and is present here with you today. The imagination helps to break the ice and start the conversation as you spend quality time with God. It works best with Scriptures that have a lot of visual description or action to them.

Preparation: *Come, Holy Spirit, enlighten the eyes of my heart.* Be present to the God who is always present to you. Call to mind his loving care for you and spend the first minute of your prayer resting in the free, unearned gift of loving and being loved. Let gratitude rise in your heart.

Set the Scene: Ask God for whatever grace it is you desire to receive in today's prayer time. Read the passage through and picture the scene in your mind. Choose the time of day and the scenery. Populate it with people dressed in period clothes. Alternatively, you can picture the scene happening in your own city or neighborhood.

Action! Read the passage a second time and play the scene forward in your mind. Notice how the participants react and what they are thinking and feeling. Notice where Jesus is and what he is doing. You can also choose to pay attention to Mary, God the Father, the Holy Spirit, or another person in the passage. Place yourself in the scene.

Acknowledge: Read the passage a third time. What does this passage stir up in your mind and heart? Pay attention to your thoughts, feelings, and desires. Don't worry if they are "correct," just notice them without any judgment.

Relate: As the scene is finished, spend some time in conversation with

Jesus. You can walk with him, sit with him in the scene, or just be aware of his presence in your prayer space. Share your thoughts, feelings, desires, and fears, honestly and openly.

Receive: How does God respond to what you have shared? What is in God's heart for you? Receiving isn't meant to be hard work. It is about relaxing into God's loving presence, focusing on him, and noticing what word, Scripture passage, feeling, or reminder God wants to give you.

Respond: This is a chance to deepen the conversation. Ask a question about what God seems to be saying, or just say, "Thank you." Like good friends, let yourself enjoy God's company for a little while.

SUGGESTIONS FOR JOURNALING

1. Something in my life that connected with the passage was …
2. As the scene played out, what struck me was …
3. I talked to Jesus about …
4. I sensed Jesus wanted to tell me, give me, or remind me …
5. I left prayer with a new insight, understanding, or call to …

After you've journaled, close with a brief conversation giving thanks to God for your prayer experience. Then pray an Our Father or another favorite prayer.

Relational Prayer (ARRR)

Relational prayer is a great way of praying with the experiences of everyday life. No matter what kinds of struggles or challenges you are facing, you can always pause and take a moment to give them to God. Here's how you do it:

Preparation: *Come, Holy Spirit, enlighten the eyes of my heart.* Be present to the God who is always present to you. Call to mind his loving care for you and spend the first minute of your prayer resting in the free, unearned gift of loving and being loved. Let gratitude rise in your heart.

Acknowledge: Notice what is going on inside of you — your thoughts, feelings, and desires. Helpful statements include, "When he did/said/acted that way, it made me feel ____."

If you are feeling too angry to concentrate, pray the name of Jesus a few times and stick with the preparation period until you notice his peaceful presence. With anger in particular, it is helpful to try and notice what you were thinking and feeling just before you got angry. That can be a clue to where the anger came from, and what God might want you to share with him.

Relate: Share with the Lord what is going on inside of you. Be honest with God. Sometimes we are mad at God himself because he appears to be ruining our lives or ignoring our prayers. You can get mad at God. Tell him how you feel, even if it includes inappropriate words. It's important that we be completely honest with him. Do not ask God to give you something or to do something at this stage. Just tell him what is going on within you.

Receive: Now we shift our attention from us and our problems to God. This is where I often got stuck when I was learning this prayer form.

Picture this scene: I'm struggling with something. A good friend comes and stands next to me. I point out the problem, tell him everything, and he listens patiently. God and I are looking at my problem together. Now, I turn to focus on my friend.

What is in his heart for me? How does he look at me? It's his turn to talk. Sometimes it's just knowing that he cares, a feeling of peace, or that I am not alone in my problem. Sometimes it might be a Scripture passage or a few words to put me in my place or add perspective. Like with any good friend, it may not be exactly what I want to hear, but it will be what I need to hear.

Respond: If what he just gave you is hard to receive, tell him so. If it comforts you, thank him. If you don't get anything at this time, you can be confident that God will give you what you really need and will answer you in his time. So keep your eyes and ears open in case he has more to say or give you later.

Sharing your burdens with God makes them melt like snow in the sunshine. It's almost like magic, but better. We call it "grace." Practice this prayer time with the experiences of your everyday life.

SUGGESTIONS FOR JOURNALING

1. My strongest thought, feeling, or emotion was …
2. I needed to share with God that …
3. God wanted me to know …
4. In the course of my prayer time, I realized that …
5. I ended prayer with a new way of thinking, acting, responding, or believing as…
6. I feel called by God to …

After you've journaled, spend a few minutes thanking God for the quality time together. Then pray an Our Father or another favorite prayer.

The Saturday Review

I like to keep an old canning jar as a "Gratitude Jar." I start at New Year's, and each Saturday I write on a slip of paper the one thing I am most grateful for that week and add it to the jar. At the end of the year, I dump out the jar and review my blessings. If you're interested in adopting this practice for yourself, a Saturday review like those we did throughout the *Oriens* pilgrimage can help fill your jar.

Preparation: *Come, Holy Spirit, enlighten the eyes of my heart.* Call to mind God's loving care for you and spend the first minute of your prayer resting in the free, unearned gift of loving and being loved. Let gratitude rise in your heart.

Flip back through your past week's journal entries. If you don't journal, cast your mind back through your week. Where did you go to Mass last Sunday? What did you receive from it? What was a high point this week? What was a low point? Here are some questions to help you:

1. My biggest blessing in the past week was …
2. My biggest challenge was …
3. Where did I notice God, and what was he doing or saying?
4. How did I respond to what God was doing?
5. I felt God's love most strongly when …
6. I'm grateful for …
7. This past week, my strongest sense, image, moment, or experience of God's loving presence was …

Journal for a little while about whatever you are experiencing.

Conclude by conversing with God about your week. Acknowledge what you have been experiencing. Relate it to him. Receive what he wants to give you. Respond to him. Then savor that image of God's loving presence and rest there for a minute or two. Close with a Glory Be.

Acknowledgments

Thank you to Our Lady, the Queen of Heaven, who appeared in Champion, Wisconsin, in 1859. Thank you to the National Shrine of Our Lady of Champion for welcoming pilgrims as a place of prayer, peace, and hospitality.

I am grateful to Tim, my first partner on pilgrimage, and all my fellow walking pilgrims through the years. Your companionship has richly blessed and encouraged me.

To Father Paul, Father Tom, Father Ryan, Father Michael, and my priestly fraternity group, Father Looney and the priests and people of the Diocese of Green Bay.

Thank you to the good people of St. John the Evangelist, Sts. Mary and Hyacinth, St. Wenceslaus, and Sts. James and Stanislaus Parishes.

Thank you to the Institute for Priestly Formation for my training as a spiritual director. This book is a fruit of their ministry, which is why I am donating my royalties to support their work. Learn more at www.priestlyformation.org.

Thank you to my loving family, especially my parents, Jim and Marion, who often tell me they love me and are proud of me.

To all the walking pilgrimage participants down through the years, especially the 7Pilgrims Group from 2022. You are a gift.

And to you, my fellow *Oriens* pilgrim. I wrote this book for you. I hope we meet some day, in this life or the next. The best is yet to come!

About the Author

Fr. Joel Sember was ordained a priest in 2007 for the Diocese of Green Bay, Wisconsin. He has extensive experience as a parish priest and two years of service in campus ministry. He made a thirty-day Ignatian silent retreat and later completed the Spiritual Direction Training Program through the Institute for Priestly Formation in Omaha, Nebraska. He holds a B.A. in philosophy and Catholic studies from the University of St. Thomas, a bachelor's in sacred theology from the Pontifical Gregorian University, and a license in sacred theology from the Pontifical University Santa Croce in Rome. He has completed a dozen walking pilgrimages. He currently serves as pastor of four parishes in rural northeastern Wisconsin.

Between ministry and parish meetings, Father Joel rides a motorcycle and paddles a kayak around great Wisconsin lakes. You can listen to his homily podcast every Sunday at pilgrimpriest.us.